PIKE
FISHING
IN THE UK
& IRELAND

PIKE
FISHING
IN THE UK
& IRELAND

Edited by Dr Steve Rogowski

Contributors: Mark Ackerley, Jon Cotton, Dick Culpin, Chris Donovan, Neville Fickling, Stephen Hincks, Steve Ormrod, Bill Palmer and Chris Turnbull

Foreword by Professor Barrie Rickards

The Crowood Press

First published in 2006 by
The Crowood Press Ltd
Ramsbury, Marlborough
Wiltshire SN8 2HR

www.crowood.com

British Library Cataloguing-in-Publication Data
A catalogue record for this book is available from the British Library

ISBN 1 86126 867 X
EAN 978 1 86126 867 9

Photograph previous page: a 20lb 4oz pike for Chris Parry from Lake
of Menteith.

Typeface used: M Plantin.

Typeset and designed by
D & N Publishing
Lambourn Woodlands, Hungerford, Berkshire.

Printed and bound in Great Britain by The Cromwell Press, Trowbridge.

CONTENTS

FOREWORD

If you are a beginner to pike angling, or a more experienced angler wanting a change or a holiday in a different area to your normal piking, then such a book as this will be a godsend. Very few of them have been available in the past – I recall only Bill Winship's *Pike Waters*, now out of date somewhat. The editors of such tomes have to strike a delicate balance between revealing too much detail about a water, which might lead to serious overfishing and resulting damage to the pike, and too general a discourse that in the end helps no one. In this volume Steve Rogowski gets the balance exactly right.

I have pike fished in most areas of the United Kingdom and Ireland, except for the south west and the Lake District of England. In fact, I have fished the Lakes a bit, but I do not know them. If I venture further in these regions then the first thing I shall do is to reread the appropriate and commendable chapters herein, with an Ordnance Survey map by my side. The only waters that are explored in a swim-by-swim detail are seriously controlled waters. For example, Neville Fickling gives excellent accounts of Blithfield and Ladybower reservoirs, but, because the pike fishing on these waters is well controlled, overfishing is less likely to result. In contrast, the first-rate chapter on the Fens by Dick Culpin is well balanced indeed; it aims to help the reader without destroying the fishing. I know the Fens well, and Dick has certainly succeeded with his contribution.

All the chapters have something important, informative and interesting to say and some are particularly exciting, such as Bill Palmer's on fishing in the south east of England and Mark Ackerley's on Ireland. When you have writers and pike anglers of this calibre, together with Steve Ormrod, Chris Donovan and Jon Cotton along with all the other contributors too, then you know that you are in for more than a 'where-to-fish' approach. All of them are careful to advise on methods and techniques, and they include memorable catches and pike fishing stories. In so doing, every one of them captures the very atmosphere of their own piking. So this is not a dry, where-to-fish book. On the contrary, it manages to convey the essence of the sport of pike fishing and is exceedingly readable and enjoyable as a result.

Barrie Rickards
Cambridge, November 2005

DEDICATION

To the memory of the late Jon Cotton.

ACKNOWLEDGEMENTS

The first persons I must mention are my father Julian Rogowski and his friend Felix. They, sometimes with my mother Shirley Rogowski, took my brother Michael and me fishing in Yorkshire all those years ago when we were young boys. Lots of pike, to double figures, were caught then, but I had to wait many years until I caught one. Others in my childhood, through teenage years and into young adulthood, following our fishing exploits on Yorkshire rivers and still-waters, also deserve a mention. They include Michael Robinson, Ken Wright, Roy Tattersfield, John Cross, Mick Peel and Mick Bebb.

I returned to fishing, and more importantly pike fishing, in early middle age and it was at the ripe age of 41 that I caught my first pike! Soon afterwards, my third almost broke the 30lb barrier so it is not really surprising that I have been gripped by pike fishing ever since. Other companionships developed over the ensuing years and these are commented on in my introductory chapter.

When it comes to the editing of this book it should be no surprise that I am fully indebted to all the contributors, along with Professor Barrie Rickards, who kindly agreed to write the foreword and made some helpful comments. Others who have helped during this project are Adam Rogowski, Richard Young, Dave Greenwood, Danny Haynes, Paul Grimsley, John Davey, Karl Highton, Mark Goddard, Steve Appleby, Stephen Doble, Jason Davies, Phil Kirk and Chris Bishop. If I have missed anyone out, my apologies to them and I hope that they will understand. Finally, I trust that the reader will enjoy this book, but it goes without saying that I take full responsibility for any mistakes or inaccuracies that may be found.

Steve Rogowski
Oldham, November 2005

1 INTRODUCTION: PIKE AND PIKE FISHING

Steve Rogowski

The pike – *Esox lucius* to give it its scientific name – is the United Kingdom's and Ireland's largest native, predatory, freshwater fish. The pike's size, up to nearly 50lb (although read about the Warren monster in Bill Palmer's chapter), and its ferocity have made it the target for many anglers hoping for that fish of a lifetime. It is a very swift, efficient and streamlined fish, these being attributes which are adaptations to its predatory lifestyle. Not surprisingly, it has been known as the 'freshwater shark' and the 'water' or 'river wolf'. There is, for example, the camouflage colouring of the green and yellow body markings, which help to disguise the pike as it lies in wait in the weeds or among tree roots. The eyes are set well forward, providing a sort of binocular vision, which makes it possible to judge distances to almost pin-point accuracy. The dorsal and the anal fins are almost aligned and set near the tail so that an extraordinary amount of power can be exerted when it propels itself towards its prey. And the head is elongated with a large mouth and lower jaw angled backwards that contains many needle-sharp teeth, which give such prey little chance of escape. There is no wonder that many of us want to pit our wit against this ferocious predator, and that some even become almost addicted to this aspect of angling.

Fishing for pike, though, is more than simply catching them. It is about escapism, leaving the stresses of everyday life behind. It is about companionships, the friendly banter and the same old jokes. It is about setting off in the early hours of the morning when the roads are empty and driving out to the countryside. Surely you cannot beat arriving at the water soon after dawn as the mist slowly rises with the need to fish welling up inside? But again, it is more than catching fish, it is about telling the difference between a swallow and a swift, a kestrel and a sparrowhawk. It is also about watching roach and dace topping everywhere before a pike suddenly strikes and scatters them in all directions. All this, of course, is not to diminish the thrill of catching fish and pike in particular. Who can forget the adrenalin rush that makes the heartbeat double when the pike float bobs before sinking into the depths? Or, after watching and waiting for hours, what better sight and sound is there other than when the bite indicator trembles and the bite alarm bleeps hesitantly before wailing away as the deadbait is snaffled? And although many of us dream of catching a 30lb fish, one must remember that even much smaller pike can give you a good scrap and that they also have a freshness and vitality that can be lacking in their larger brethren.

I begin this chapter with some general discussion of pike lore, including its life and habitats, along with some of the thrills to be gained from catching these hard-fighting fish. This is followed by a brief discussion about the methods used to catch them. As alluded to, I also look at the associated aspects of such fishing, such as the companionships involved and the wonders of nature, not least its fascinating fauna and flora and beautiful scenery. Although such sights often arise when you are pike fishing in more secluded countryside, rather bleak and depressing urban or semi-urban waters can provide interesting delights. Finally, I relate all of the foregoing to the following chapters in this book.

'Secretive' Dave Greenwood with a 31lb 6oz specimen from a northern still-water.

BELOW: *But pike fishing is not just about big pike; snappers like this have a freshness and vitality often lacking in their larger brethren.*

Pike Lore

When it comes to our knowledge of the pike, at the outset it must be said that that there are many myths surrounding old esox. For example, the famous Mannheim pike was said to be 267 years old (AD1230–1497) when, in reality, a pike might not live much more than 20 years. There has also been many a story about waters throughout the United Kingdom and Ireland, which are said to be inhabited by a 'monster pike'. Invariably the weight of such a fish is put at about 60 or even 70lb, with people talking of its attacking horses and cows as they drink! For example, a giant pike that ruled Whittlesea Mere in Cambridgeshire for many years was even said to be over 80lb. However, when the mere was drained in 1851 it was found to weigh 52lb and even then there is some doubt about its authenticity. More recently, one has only to recall that Ropner Park Lake, Stockton was reputed to have a 'monster pike' that devoured ducklings and signets, but when it was drained in 2005 there was no sign of it. So it must be remembered that many such stories are precisely that and should be always be taken with a pinch of salt. However, staying with size, more believable is John Garvin's 53lb from Lough Conn in 1920, and Tommy Morgan's 47lb from Loch Lomand in 1945. In reality, pike in the United Kingdom and Ireland do grow to well over 40lb although such fish are hard to come by, and even a 30lb pike is beyond the reach of most anglers. Of course, this does not stop us all continuing to try.

Pike are widespread in lowland rivers and still-waters such as lakes, reservoirs, gravel pits, canals and drains. They can survive some pollution and low oxygen content as well as very low temperatures, but high temperatures can prove fatal. Generally they do not thrive in oligotrophic (nutrient-poor) waters, such as highland waters, which are often acidic when small, nor in fast-flowing, spate rivers. They are largely solitary fish, but not territorial, although you can catch several pike from the same hotspot. This is probably because they are there for the prey fish rather than their massing together instinctively as a shoal. Most of their time is spent in deeper water from 10 to 30ft, but from February to March onwards they move to the shallows to spawn. There will be the large females and smaller males, the latter rarely growing larger than 10lb in weight. The females will then produce eggs and the bigger ones, of say 20lb and over, will produce more than 500,000 eggs each spring, though many are swallowed by such as waterfowl before they hatch out. When a female has been hooked at this time of the year it is not uncommon to see a couple of small males follow her to the bank. At other times of the year the latter would have provided a nice meal.

After spawning, pike go on a feeding frenzy for a couple of months or so. Females again feed heavily in October–November when their ovaries are beginning to develop, and there is another peak in feeding before spawning. A pike's basic diet consists almost entirely of fish and will comprise whatever species is the commonest in the water. Young pike, the jacks, will eat water fleas and other tiny aquatic life, but they soon move on to fry and small fish in general. They are generally fast growing, with the males and the females maturing in two to three years. As indicated, pike are also cannibalistic and a large female will readily eat a pike of several pounds or so. Other vertebrate creatures living in or on the water, such as waterfowl, frogs and small mammals, are not immune. I once saw a frog in the margins of a remote Scottish loch that was obviously wounded and had no back legs, perhaps the obvious explanation being that a pike had grabbed it.

After spawning in the shallows, where do the pike spend the rest of the year? A short answer is where the prey fish can be found. They can grow quickly, perhaps up to 4lb a year, though this is geared to the food supply available. Sometimes one will hide in weed and reed beds, for example, or under the stump of an overhanging tree, waiting for unsuspecting roach or perch to pass. Then, with a lash of its powerful tail, the victim is captured and engulfed in the huge mouth from where there is little chance of escape. Alternatively, the bigger pike may decide that skulking around in ambush is not for them. When they decide to feed they make a field day of it, moving out into open water and plundering shoals of prey fish.

So why are so many people determined and dedicated to trying to catch this fascinating and ferocious fish? Part of the reason is the pike's very ferocity; using rather extravagant language, it really is a foe that is worthy of its steel. To tempt, hook, play and land a good-sized pike calls for considerable skill. There will be the solid feel as the rod is almost bent double and a large 'mama' sends out the message 'don't mess!' The surges and runs can test the best tackle as well as the keenest and most experienced angler. As suggested, even jacks provide excellent sport, especially on lighter tackle. These and even larger pike can provide epic scraps, which include actions such as tail-walking with gaping jaws as attempts are made to shake the hooks free.

Being involved in all of this is something that only pikers can really appreciate, with their friends, partners and family often thinking there is something amiss with them, whether it be some defect in their genes, personalities or lives. Perhaps all of these factors have a role to play, but surely really it is all to do with using your knowledge and skills to outwit these wily predators. There is also the sense of being in competition with 'nature', since, apart from the pike themselves, there are also their location and the weather to consider. But be all that as it may, the key questions are: how do you catch them and what methods do you use?

John Davey with a fine 25lb 12oz from Rudyard Lake, Staffordshire. It snaffled a drifted dead dace.

Almost a 20, Steve Rogowski with a reservoir 19lb 12oz, which gave a terrific account of itself.

Methods for Catching Pike

These are referred to throughout this book, and in much more detail than here. At this stage I merely provide a basic outline of the three main methods of pike fishing, namely livebaiting, deadbaiting and lure fishing.

At the outset the importance of having the correct tackle has to be emphasized and to this end specialist rods are required. For live or deadbaiting a pike rod of 11 or 12ft, or even 13 if fishing at distance, together with a 2½ to 3½lb test curve is required. These can easily handle casting small livebaits and big deadbaits, as well as landing large pike. A strong reel is also necessary, one that can take line in the 14 to 18lb bracket. Despite the advent of braid, and being a bit of a piking dinosaur, I still tend to use monofilament. I also prefer fixed spool reels rather than the various closed-face or multiplier reels. If the intention is to ledger using a float or to suspend the bait in the water, then a sliding pike float is

required, this being held in position by a stop knot and bead above the float. Paternoster booms can also be used if one is going to suspend a bait adjacent to a feature, in which case either a float or a sunken float is also used. Ledger weights or leads are also required and the line must have a wire up-trace before being connected by a swivel to an approximately 18in wire trace proper, of around 15 to 20lb or 30lb test. Two treble hooks of say, size eight or six, depending on the size of the bait, are then attached. Other essential items of tackle include, for example, banksticks/rod rests, electronic bite alarms, drop-back indicators, a large landing net, forceps for unhooking your catch, an unhooking mat, a weigh sling and, not least, weighing scales and a camera for, you hope, that fish of a lifetime. Finally, we need the live or deadbaits. As for the former, then virtually any coarse fish – for instance, roach, perch, ruffe, bream, dace, gudgeon, chub or bleak, as well as brown or rainbow trout – will catch pike. As for deads, any of these coarse fish as well as eels (in sections) work well. Smelt are also good baits; although they are migratory fish of the sea, they can be caught in the lower reaches of rivers during spring when they enter freshwater to spawn. Similar comments can be made about the lamprey, which is an equally good deadbait (again in sections). In addition to coarse deads, sea deads, for example, mackerel, herring, sardine, sprats and sandeels, are excellent baits, probably because, as well as appealing to the pike's keen eyesight, they also appeal to its highly developed sense of smell. They are used as whole baits or can be chopped in half, depending on their size.

All of the foregoing refers largely to bank fishing for pike, although you can, of course, and many do, boat fish for them. I do little of it myself and would not presume to advise others in detail. However, I would say that you do need a boat and hull design which is suited to the type of water you are fishing, whether it is the Norfolk Broads or the large expanses such as the Irish loughs. Displacement hulls push through the water at a slow rate but are very stable, being ideal for small waters. Semi-planing hulls partly come out of water under power, giving speed and good stability. Finally, planing hulls come right out of the water giving great speed and being necessary for large expanses of water where rapid movement from one area to another is required. Whatever your choice, a boat length of about 14ft is ideal for pike fishing, and then you will need a suitable outboard motor, anchors, ropes and, ideally, a fish-finder.

Turning to livebaiting, there are five main techniques. First, free roving/roaming a livebait – suspending a livebait below a float that allows the bait to swim around – has already been referred to and is an exciting way to catch pike. A lot of water can be covered, thereby increasing the chances of your bait coming to the attention of a pike. A point to note is that, unless you are using floating braid, the line should be greased to stop it sinking. The bait is hooked by inserting the bottom treble into the root of the pectoral fin, beneath the bait's gills. The second treble is then inserted at the root of the dorsal fin on the bait's back. However, I often prefer lip hooking the bait

with a single treble, thus ensuring that it retains its action for much longer. It may mean that a few jacks could be lost but the bigger pike will readily be caught.

Second, ledgering livebaits can be a very effective means of catching pike. Float ledgering has also already been mentioned, but equally a basic running ledgered livebait is equally likely to succeed. For both, the bottom treble is inserted halfway down the side of the body, while the second treble goes into the tail root. Such a rig can be successful on clear bottomed waters if you position the bait in an area where the pike are likely to patrol, such as the bottom of a drop-off.

Third, paternostered livebaiting, as suggested, involves tethering the bait above the water bottom by using a boom and a surface or subsurface (sunken float paternoster) float and a ledger weight/lead. The bait is also mounted on a shorter trace, this ensuring that it does not tangle with the rest of the rig. Again, I prefer a single treble which lip-hooks the bait, which is then positioned near where pike are likely to lay up, for example, in weed or reed beds and beneath overhanging trees and bushes.

Fourth, drifting livebaits involve the use of a specialist drifter float with a vane which is attach-ed to a ledger weight/lead and the wire trace. The bait is hooked on to the trace, as with free-roving livebaits. The wind being behind you, it pushes the vane, which moves the rig and the bait through the water, enabling a great area of water to be covered, as well as areas that could not be cast to from the bank. You can even explore areas where it is likely that pike have never seen a bait. Again, unless you are using floating braid, the line must be greased to prevent it from sinking.

And fifth, trolling involves slowly dragging baits behind a moving boat. At its simplest, float trolling requires a sliding float being held in position by a stop knot and bead above the float. Beneath the float there is a ledger weight or lead and a wire trace. The bottom treble is inserted in the side of the bait near the vent and the second one is lip hooked; this is important because, if it is inserted otherwise, the bait could be drowned by being trolled backwards. A good tip is to alter constantly the depths at which the baits are set until feeding pike are found.

Pike are hunters and predators and so it is not surprising that livebaiting can lead to many a pike being caught. But it is worth emphasizing that, like other predators, pike are active scavengers and as such deadbaiting is probably the most widely used method of catching them. There are two techniques for this, namely, the static and the mobile.

At its simplest, static deadbaiting involves the running ledger and float ledger rigs, although paternostered (float and sunken float) deadbaits can also be used. Essentially, they are the same rigs as for ledgering and paternostering livebaits and are used in much the same way. Even with the larger baits, which can be cut in half, the trebles are again inserted much as you would if you were using livebaits. A popped-up deadbait is a variant of the running ledger rig with, for

Steve Rogowski with a nice 15lb 2oz that fell to a sunken paternostered dead roach.

example, foam inserted inside the dead bait so it floats off the bottom and can be more easily seen by pike. It can be effective where a weedy bottom or soft mud is likely to hide the bait. Paternostered deadbaits are also particularly useful if the bottom is weedy.

When it comes to mobile deadbaiting, here you are not just focusing on the pike's highly developed sense of sight and smell, but also its sensitivity to vibrations. Many a time I have seen a pike lying silently and seemingly lethargically in the margins, but on, for example, reeling in a swim feeder, as soon as the latter comes within the pike's vibration range, it will quickly become alert, turn and swim inquisitively to see what is going on. There are three aspects of mobile deadbaiting to note, namely, wobbling, drifter float deadbaiting and trolling.

Wobbling, or, as some prefer to call it, sinking and drawing, is, in effect, spinning with a dead fish. It is hooked head-up on the trace and then cast and retrieved in an enticing manner. It can be used, for instance, in locating pike on a particular water by walking round and casting as you go; it is also worth a try when a pike is seen attacking prey fish. You really need a tough deadbait for wobbling and so it is often that baits such as perch, mackerel or trout are used, although, of course, on occasions softer fish are worth a try. And even half a fish, such as a mackerel head or tail, can be effective.

Drifter float deadbaiting is similar to drifter float livebaiting, although the hooks are inserted as for ledgered livebaits, namely, the bottom treble halfway down the side of the body and the second treble in the root of the tail. They are particularly useful for searching out likely looking pike holding areas rather than just concentrating on your own swim.

Trolling with deadbaits is, again, largely much the same as trolling with livebaits. But, in addition, this is where bouncing a deadbait along the bottom can come into its own. Simply put the rig consists of a half-moon lead placed above the trace. The bait, and, again, preferably a tough bait, is then hooked head up and you are ready to go.

Moving to lure fishing, it really can be an exhilarating way of catching pike and, even though their average size may be smaller, you can still get the bigger specimens. You are also likely to get more fish. The rod should be about 9ft for bank fishing, although when on a boat or on a small drain a 6ft rod will suffice. A test curve of about 1¾ to 2lb with a stiff action is ideal. As for reels, again I prefer fixed spool reels to multipliers, with the line being in the range of 10 to 15lb. I know braid is all the rage at the moment but I remain committed to monofilament. Wire traces should be 12in long, with a swivel on one end and a link swivel at the other. And much of the tackle needed for livebaiting and deadbaiting, not least the landing net and forceps, are also required. We then come to the lures themselves and here we really are spoilt for choice. There are hundreds of lures to choose from and here I merely comment on some of them, in particular, the main categories.

One of the oldest types of lure is the spoon, which is actually derived from the common table-spoon. They weave and wobble in the water, thus triggering the pike's predatory instinct. Although I favour the simplicity of a silver or copper Atlantic spoon, manufacturers have now stretched and twisted spoons and also decorated them with such as eyes, stripes and various colours. The larger spoons are good for trolling and, although the traditional Atlantic-type spoon is difficult to cast into the wind, others, such as the Toby, can easily remedy the situation.

Spinning blades on lures attract pike and thus spinners and spinnerbaits, the latter having blades away from the body of the lure, are a must for the tackle box of any lure fisher. Although many spinners are a little small for pike, the largest Mepps and Mepps-like spinners are certainly worth using. They are probably better in shallower water and in water that has good visibility, whereas spinnerbaits seem to do better in deeper, cloudier water.

Plugs are essentially artificial fish and they come in several types. Surface plugs, as the name suggests, float on the surface, requiring their action to be imparted by the angler and it is hard to beat the sight of a pike engulfing one of these lures. Poppers and chuggers, for example, have blunt 'faces', maximizing the water resistance and causing the plug to bubble and spit in response to jerks in the rod tip. Prop-baits have a propeller-like spinner at their head and tail, and water pressure causes these to rotate and churn up spray, thus attracting pike. And crawlers flip-flop across the surface, usually by means of a double-lobed lip.

Crankbaits are diving plugs, which are given their action by means of a lip or diving vane; the reel handle has only to be 'cranked' to make them work. Plugs with little diving vanes at close to right angles to their length run shallow, while those with big lips closer to parallel with their length run deep. I often prefer the short, fat-bellied, stubby tail of the Shakespeare 'Big S' because of its rolling, wobbling action, which readily produces pike. There are also proportionally longer and laterally compressed shad plugs and the elongated minnow. Finally, there are lipless crankbaits, such as rattlebaits, which are vibrating, noisy and fast-sinking plugs.

Mention should be made of the increasing popularity of the 'rubbery' swimbaits and replicants, which often look and feel like real fish. They are very popular in the USA as are jerk-baits, which were originally used mainly for catching musky, an aggressive relative of the pike. Unlike many conventional lures, they have

Dawn on a reservoir and 'Spinning' Steve Appleby is hard at it.

no lips and so the angler has to jerk the rod in order to impart life into the lure. And generally a shorter, stiffer rod is needed rather than conventional lure rods.

Finally, a comment about fly fishing for pike. It has been around for a long time but seems to be becoming more popular, although to be honest I have yet to attempt it. Briefly, basic tackle involves a rod capable of casting large flies on a 9 or 10 line, fly lines, monofilament leaders, wire traces, some flies and the rest of your pike tackle, such as forceps, landing net and the like.

Pike-Fishing Companions

To catch pike successfully you have to have some knowledge of the pike itself as well as of the several methods and techniques. Having briefly dealt with these, we now come to the companionships involved in fishing for them. At the outset it must be said that many, including myself, are quite happy to fish on their own. One piking acquaintance even told me that 'little or nothing misses the eye of the lone piker'. I guess the implication is that perhaps one is more likely to be alert to what is happening around you, including in and on the water, if you are on your own. But surely fishing in good company cannot be surpassed. There are the shared successes and failures to be had, the friendly competition and, not least, the shared laughs and jokes. To a greater or lesser extent all the contributors to this book echo such a view.

Being born and bred in Leeds, much of my early fishing was spent on Yorkshire rivers such as the Ure and the Wharfe, when my brother Mike and I used to go on fishing escapades with our father and his friend. Mike and I were usually content to float fish and catch the like of small perch, roach and gudgeon, while dad and his friend would be catching lots of jacks together with the occasional double. On occasions we would go night fishing for eels, with many being caught on ledgered worms and minnows. These early years of my fishing, the late 1950s and the early 1960s, provide fond memories, which

include long summer days and evenings with lots of fish being caught.

Later on, with teenage friends, we would fish on our own at local ponds as well as venues a little further afield as on rivers such as the Aire and Wharfe. And while Mike had already caught his first pike, including a fine thirteen-pounder from the Ure, I had yet to catch one. Into young adulthood, during the 1970s and the 1980s, fishing largely took a back seat as I became increasingly preoccupied by the hedonistic lifestyle induced by student life spent at several universities. It was a period dominated by alcohol, socializing, rock music and members of the opposite sex. But, as is usually the case, you cannot completely keep fishing out of your life, even though it was not until the early 1990s that the fishing, or as it turned out, the piking bug returned.

I guess that it was for old times' sake that Carl Wood and I returned to the Ure. We caught lots of perch, some over 2lb, as well as such as eels, gudgeon, roach and small chub. But it was a 2½lb jack that I caught on a floated live gudgeon, my first pike, that made the day. Soon after I caught another, before catching my third at a small still-water in Greater Manchester. It fell to a ledgered sprat and weighed in at a superb 29lb 4oz, and, unsurprisingly, I have been hooked on piking ever since.

By the mid-1990s Mike and I also returned to our old haunt on the Ure, this time with his two sons Adam and Tim. Such visits used to entail camping overnight, lighting fires and catching more eels as well as pike. Adam, after a spell of really being into fly fishing with his dad and brother, has gradually 'got into' piking, eventually getting some nice fish into the bargain.

Karl 'King of the Jacks' Highton and Mark Goddard are two more recent piking partners, along with 'Spinning' Steve Appleby. Then there is the new kid on the block, Richard Young. They have caught many double and 20lb pike between them, but the pike-fishing sessions with them, and all the others mentioned above, have been a lot more than catching pike. For instance, I tend to think a special part of pike fishing is the sharing aspect. You might share a

Steve Rogowski's third pike and still a personal best weighing in at 29lb 4oz. A ledgered sprat did the trick.

beer or a sandwich and then, when one of you does catch, you are sharing it with the other because he will net it for you. It is also important to be philosophical when you do not catch. A good time is still had as you chat and muck about, laughing and joking. There are also more serious discussions about, for example, lives, careers and even how we might change the world.

Back to Nature

In addition to the companionships involved in pike fishing, when one is out on the water there is the feeling of being close to nature. What can beat relaxing, away from the stresses of work, in peaceful and beautiful surroundings, often with the chance of seeing some fascinating wildlife? A few examples of this readily spring to mind. One of my favourite areas for pike fishing is the Lake District. There is an incredible variety of breathtaking scenery crammed into a relatively small area. There are green dales, cobbled towns, the stark Cumbrian mountains and, not least as far as pike fishing is concerned, mirror-surfaced lakes often

surrounded by woodland. Often, particularly as dawn breaks, it is possible to see roe and fallow deer, and on one occasion I was even lucky enough to see a badger.

Pike fishing on Scottish lochs, whether in Dumfries and Galloway or the Highlands, is also hard to beat. There are, of course, the beautiful lochs but also rugged mountains, glens and heather-clad moors all of which are home to such creatures as otters, red deer and golden eagles. I recall, for example, sitting on the banks of Loch Ronald and watching a playful otter preening itself in the shallows, or, while on Woodhall Loch, there was the magnificent sight of a recently reintroduced red kite soaring high above me. Yorkshire rivers may not now be surrounded by the meadowland of old, over the last fifty years such traditional grassland has disappeared due to changed farming practices, but this does not mean that there is no interesting wildlife to observe. Rabbits are common, as are pheasants and, if you are lucky, it is possible even to see a hare. In summer butterflies and grasshoppers abound and, even if they are somewhat threatened, the warbling song of the skylark can still be heard. Finally, even when pike fishing on a cold, windswept north of England reservoir, nature reveals herself in many ways. It could simply be the company so often provided by a friendly robin with its red breast and cheerful song, or the sight of a gaggle of Canada geese flying overhead before landing on the water as one; even the sight of a friendly, inquisitive swan is surely something to behold.

So, pike fishing is more than simply catching pike, much as we all want to do that, it is also about hearing the sound of a distant cuckoo or seeing a kingfisher flying up and down the river on a hot summer's day. It is about watching a shoal of bleak gobbling up midges before they are scattered by a small, charging perch. In short, it is also about appreciating the sights and sounds of nature and I am sure that all the contributors to this book would, to a greater or lesser extent, agree with such a view.

The Book

This brings me to the book itself. As the title states, it is about pike fishing in the United Kingdom and Ireland and thus each chapter has a geographical or regional focus. The whole of the United Kingdom and Ireland are covered, albeit this does not mean that every significant pike water or even every area is dealt with. For example, Jon Cotton deals with the south west of England, while Bill Palmer deals with the south east. But where do the south west and the south east end? Arguably it is somewhere in Hampshire, but neither contributor actually refers to this county so a major pike river such as the Avon barely gets a mention. Then when it comes to the north of England, Stephen Hincks deals with the Lake District while I deal with northern reservoirs (with Steve Ormrod) and the Yorkshire rivers, but pike waters in the north east hardly get a mention. Part of the explanation for this is that, perhaps, the north east is not as renowned for its pike fishing as other parts of the country. But, in any case, I am sure that the reader will agree and appreciate that it is simply not possible to cover every possible pike water. Indeed, this is not the

aim of the book, rather it is to give an overall flavour of the pike fishing opportunities in these countries and this is what all the contributors have attempted to do. So let us look at their chapters in a little more detail.

Despite the appearance of large pike from trout reservoirs, perhaps the best chance of catching a large pike in Britain remains with the Norfolk Broads. Chris Turnbull provides an overview of opportunities in this unique area of England. Actually, he starts by commenting on the degradation of the Broads' ecology over recent decades, arguing that the golden era of piking has passed. He even suggests that if you want a chance of a 30 or 40lb pike the trout reservoirs are indeed the places to be. But he then takes a more optimistic view of the fishing on the Broads with a tour of the waters and a discussion of the methods he uses, advising the reader that a boat is essential if you want to be serious about piking here.

The Fens have also got an excellent reputation for pike and Dick Culpin looks at the fishing here, another unique area. He acknowledges that many of the rivers and drains can be virtually featureless, so it is difficult to know where to start. However, he provides helpful advice with regard to locating pike before discussing the methods that have led him to success. He also stresses that being out on the Fenland rivers and drains is more than just about the pike fishing, there is also the animal and bird life to consider, and he recounts some amusing incidents that have occurred along the way of his piking career. Finally, despite some concerns he points out that the future for pike fishing in the Fens looks positive.

The Midlands of England cover a large area and thus a wide variety of pike-fishing opportunities. There are the drains of Lincolnshire, numerous rivers and canals, large reservoirs, lakes and gravel pits, as well as probably hundreds of ponds and other still-waters. However, in his chapter Neville Fickling concentrates on three big pike waters, namely the Blithfield and the Ladybower reservoirs and the River Trent. He provides a written tour of the former two, both of which produce pike to well over 30lb, before looking at some of his favourite venues on the Trent. The captures of some large pike are covered, together with tips and advice.

Yorkshire river pike might not be the biggest in the United Kingdom and Ireland, with 20lb fish being hard to catch and thirty-pounders being very rare. However, they are hard-fighting and provide excellent sport, often in beautiful countryside, as I hope my chapter shows. This includes a description of the main pike rivers in Yorkshire, not least the Ouse. When to go and the location of pike are dealt with, as are rigs, tactics and baits. Despite some suggestions that the Ouse has declined as a pike river, I end on an optimistic note by describing a great day's fishing I had there with one of my piking partners.

I have already referred to the natural beauty of the Lake District, and Stephen Hincks deals with the pike fishing here. He starts by showing how he 'got into' pike fishing as a schoolboy and how he caught his first 20lb pike. He goes on to deal with his preferred method of fishing, namely lure fishing the large lakes from a boat. Bank fishing and his pike-fishing companionships are also dealt with. Finally, he provides a useful introduction to pike fishing on some of the main lakes, while also acknowledging that small tarns, rivers and even canals should not be ignored.

The reservoirs of northern England may not be as productive as those in the south east, and these bleak waters can be difficult to pike fish successfully, but the positives to be gained from cracking them cannot be denied, as Steve Ormrod and I show. The emphasis is on locating the pike and the methods to employ as well as comments on how to tackle a reservoir for the first time.

Pike fishing in the English south east can be some of the best, not least because of the chance of 30 and 40lb fish from large reservoirs and gravel pits. It is these waters that Bill Palmer concentrates on. Although many of the reservoirs have ceased to stock trout, thus indicating that the chance of catching such pike has lessened, Bill thinks that the possibility remains. He deals with many of the waters he has pike fished over the years, emphasizing some memorable catches and the companionships involved before commenting on methods, rigs and baits.

Chris Donovan and Jon Cotton deal, respectively, with pike fishing in Wales and the south west of England in their chapters. Chris concentrates on South Wales, where he has fished successfully for many years, such as on Llangorse Lake and at Llandegfedd, as well as the rivers Wye and Severn, but there are also venues such as Bala Lake and the River Dee in the north to consider. Jon focuses on the pike-fishing opportunities round Bristol through Somerset to Devon, and not least the Chew Valley Reservoir and waters such as the Somerset Levels. Again, some memorable catches are included and each author provides helpful advice on how to tackle his individual area.

Pike fishing in the magnificent scenery of Scotland can be unsurpassable and this is what Steve Ormrod covers. He provides a brief guide to some of the main waters and, not surprisingly, concentrates on the lochs while also pointing out that the rivers and canals should not be ignored. Some memorable catches are included together with general advice on tactics and what to look for when trying to catch the beautifully marked, hard-fighting, Scottish pike.

Last, but certainly not least, we come to Ireland, which has always had a reputation for producing monster pike. Despite some concerns such as gill netting on the western loughs, Mark Ackerley points out that the pike fishing can be very good and not least on the big waters he likes to tackle. He concentrates on bait and lure fishing from a boat, providing helpful guidance on such fishing in the process. He ends by describing a recent memorable day's fishing that led to a new Irish personal best.

Taken together then, this book has something to say to everyone who is interested in pike and pike fishing, whether they are enthusiastic beginners after jacks and double-figure pike or more experienced anglers aiming for 20, 30 or even 40lb fish. For instance, those wanting to try pike fishing in the varied and different waters of the British Isles, those who want advice and tips on tackle, rigs and methods, and those who simply want to read about memorable catches will all find something of interest.

2 BROADLAND PIKE

Chris Turnbull

If one area in the United Kingdom can claim to be its pike angling Mecca, it is the Norfolk Broads. Where else can boast such a rich pike-fishing history, encompassing the exploits of generations of celebrated pike anglers? Included in this history is the dim and distant reputed capture of a 42lb pike by J. Nudd from Wroxham Broad in 1901, and another potential record weighing 39lb 5oz, apparently taken by Edward Spall from Martham South Broad in the 1950s. Then there are the exploits of eminent figures such as Jim Vincent and his son Edwin, and, perhaps the most controversial of all pike anglers of that time, Dennis Pye who claimed to have caught 250 pike over 20lb, of which at least a few are suspected to be figments of his imagination. There are also the well-documented exploits during the Broads' heyday of anglers such as Frank Wright and that endearing duo Reg Sandys and Bill Giles, not least because it is Bill who is credited with originating static deadbaiting. But top of this list would certainly be Peter Hancock's capture of a British record weighing 40lb 1oz, from Horsey Mere in 1967.

More recently a new generation of anglers have cut themselves a place in pike angling's hall of fame during the 1980s Broads revival. Included among these are Neville Fickling's capture of a new 41lb 6oz British record from the Thurne in 1985 and Derrick Amies's subsequent capture of the same fish at 42lb 2oz. While less eminently famous, no less spectacular were the achievements of the secretive, local angler Billy Florey, who in one season took fifty-six pike over 20lb from Martham Broad, the biggest of which weighed 37lb. This list is not complete without including the names of such as Steve Harper and Eddie Turner.

Despite these exploits, a look at the history and ecology of the Broads reveals a more sobering picture of pike fishing today. However, after dealing with such matters I then take a more optimistic view of current pike-fishing opportunities, providing a brief tour of the Broads, emphasizing the need for a boat and discussing issues of access. Finally, I look at some of the methods and techniques that I favour, including some memorable catches.

History and Ecology

Situated in the low-lying expanses of east Norfolk and north-east Suffolk, Broadland comprises the catchment area of numerous tidal rivers that collectively drain into the sea at Great Yarmouth and Lowestoft. Situated along these rivers stretch a number of open areas of water known as the Broads, most of which are connected to the main rivers while others are landlocked. It is generally accepted that the Broads are the flooded remains of peat diggings excavated in the Middle Ages. While not natural in origin, they form a unique ecological area that has become valued as an important national treasure and now given much needed protection by receiving National Park status.

How much the history and ecology of the Broads mean to pike anglers visiting the area is open to debate. To some extent it will depend on what time of the year they come since undoubtedly the Broads have two faces. In summer they are a popular tourist area, overrun by hire cruisers and yachts where it is difficult to escape the hustle. But, come winter, the Broads take on a totally different veneer, becoming a lonely wilderness

A traditional Broads vista of sky and water, Duck Broad off Heigham Sound. It might look rather bland but peace and tranquillity are often close by.

where it is still possible to spend an entire day in solitude. True, the Broads may lack the dramatic wildness of the Lake District or the Scottish lochs, but it cannot be denied that, once afloat in their more remote areas, they are a truly special place to be. Anyone who can spend the day lost in the windswept expanses of the upper Thurne Broads without feeling the magic of the place must have a very shallow soul. There, alone under the vast Norfolk sky surrounded by open water and whispering reed beds, accompanied by flittering groups of bearded tits, endless flights of wildfowl and the occasional majestic marsh harrier hunting the reed-beds, it is easy to feel at one with nature.

Such sentiments may seem overly romantic, but there is something age-old and spiritual about humankind's place in the Broads landscape. Without countless generations of human endeavour transforming it into the landscape of today, much of it would consist of salt marshes and impenetrable reed swamp. Not so long ago, for example, many of the local populace consisted of 'marshmen' who eked a livelihood out of the Broads by netting eels, shooting wildfowl and harvesting reed for thatching. Many of them would also have fished for pike, admittedly more

for the table than for sport, but I expect that these men cherished their time fishing much as we do today. Sadly, much of this way of life was ended on the battlefields of World War I. Few of Norfolk's sons returned to continue the traditional lifestyles that had once shaped the Broads. With many of the open reed marshes no longer being harvested, areas eventually became overgrown by alder carr, although on much of the Thurne and the Ant traditional reed harvesting preserves the traditional, open landscape even today.

One cannot help but dream about what the fishing would have been like on the Broads in years gone by. Not least in the heydays spanning the 1950s and the 1960s, the numbers of fish present were simply staggering and it was justly recognized as having the finest fishing in the country. You could easily bag up catching bream, rudd, roach and perch. Not surprisingly, pike also did extremely well, especially on the Thurne system where the pike fishing was simply fantastic. Good as the pike fishing can still be at times, it is a shadow of what it was back then.

Today the state of the fish stocks reflects the general degradation of the Broads environment, behind which lie a number of contributory factors. First is the eutrophication of the water brought about by phosphate enrichment from detergents in treated sewage effluent. This means that for much of the year the water is often thick with algal blooms that cut out light penetration, restricting aquatic plant growth and limiting the entire ecology. Over successive winters the algae have died off and fallen to the bottom, resulting in a thick sludge of phosphate-rich silt. While in recent years phosphate stripping has taken place at many sewage treatment works, high levels of it still remain in many beds, leaching back out and preventing the water from returning to its previous good quality.

Nowadays the Broads Authority is busily mud-pumping several of the Broads to remove phosphates. In order to work effectively, however, this procedure requires the support of biomanipulation techniques to increase the quantity of water fleas and other zooplankton that feed on algae. The main thrust of this process involves the removal of small fish that feed on zooplankton. On some Broads this has necessitated the removal of most of the roach and rudd, while on others, clear-water areas are being maintained by netting them off to keep fish out. While the science behind this is good, the practice is yet to be wholly successful except in a few landlocked Broads.

Intensive agriculture in a number of areas means that chemicals drain into the Broads and this has also contributed to this degradation. On the Thurne, for instance, nutrients being pumped into the water via numerous land drainage pumps is leading to degradation of the reed bed with large areas of reed margins and islands simply being blown away.

Biomanipulation coupled with changes in farming and sewage-treatment techniques might eventually reverse the process of eutrophication, but, unfortunately, the problems that threaten the fish stocks do not end there. Rising sea levels around the Norfolk coast are resulting in increasingly destructive saline tides surging far inland into the rivers. Fish are killed in most winters and it is not unusual for pike to take the brunt as they seem less inclined to flee as the salinity increases.

Being as close to the sea as they are, a number of the Broads have always been vulnerable to salt

water, not least the Thurne ones. The ecology brought about by the salinity of the Thurne system is unique, but for the fish there are mixed blessings. The huge abundance of brine shrimp present is certainly capable of sustaining large numbers of quality fish, which, in turn, promote massive growth in its resident pike. However, this salinity also encourages the growth of a rare toxin-producing alga *Prymnesium parvum* that can have a devastating effect on freshwater fish, resulting in high mortalities. *Prymnesium* has probably always been present on the Thurne, but in 1969 it was directly responsible for the deaths

It is 1984 and a young-looking Chris Turnbull has a fine brace of 27lb 8oz and 23lb 2oz from the Thurne at Potter Heigham.

of hundreds of thousands of fish on Hickling Broad and Horsey Mere. This created a scene of total devastation, not helped by further outbreaks between 1970 and 1975. For the anglers of that tragic time, including many mentioned earlier, it must have seemed like the end of their world; as far as the fishing was concerned for them the Thurne was dead and its Broads remained deserted for many years.

After years of neglect the Thurne gradually made a comeback, resulting in the golden years of the early 1980s. Since then, however, *Prymnesium* has intermittently reared up again, knocking the pike stocks back. The most recent serious outbreak occurred during the winter of 2000/01 and once again pike stocks on the system are low.

Putting aside ecological factors, one of the biggest causes for the present slump in stocks is simply that there are too many people fishing for them. Not so long ago, if stocks declined in one area, the fishing pressure simply moved elsewhere, but now few areas get the opportunity to recover. Twenty years ago few of us fished for pike much before 1 October, but now bait and lure fishing take place throughout the summer months. I argue for the abandonment of summer pike fishing on the Broads because this would eventually improve pike stocks considerably. I know many agree, but as the Broads are, for the main part, tidal-water, there is no statutory framework within which this can be done.

Pike-Fishing Opportunities

Having taken a somewhat sombre look at the Broads environment, let us take a more upbeat one at the pike fishing here; after all, despite much of the above, the area can still produce some excellent catches.

I moved to Norfolk in 1980 and the first thing I learned is that, while the odd bit of bank space exists, anyone who is serious about his fishing will need a boat that he can transport, otherwise he will be restricted to fishing areas where dinghies are available for hire. I like something

that is both stable and at the same time capable of moving reasonably quickly in the water. Although in the past I have risked all in unstable, little dinghies, it really is not a good idea. A 12 to 14ft glassfibre or alloy model, with a semi-planing hull, is a far better bet. You will also need a decent petrol outboard of not less than 3 or 4hp, which is not so long in the shaft that it cannot travel through shallow water. For quietly getting in and out of swims, an electric outboard with at least a 30lb thrust is a worthwhile addition. Electric outboards are also terrific for trolling, but doing this with any sort of outboard is unfortunately illegal on the Broads.

As for fixtures and fittings, it is not sensible to go afloat without a life jacket. A pair of heavy mud-weights is also essential since being unable to hold out in open water without slipping anchor is a real bind; plenty of rope on them is also an advantage, especially in the deeper tidal reaches. A pair of long oars and reliable rowlocks are also necessary. Padding the floor with carpet underlay is recommended; not only will this considerably help to reduce banging about, it will also prevent pike from scuffing up on the bottom of the boat. Carpeting does not necessarily negate the use of an unhooking mat though, which, when not in proper use, can double up as a comfortable cushion to sit on. While not essential, sprung cleats and adjustable boat rests also help to make the experience of fishing afloat that bit more enjoyable.

A view from the boat on Hickling Broad.

As for sonar, it is far less used in the generally shallow waters of Broadland, where it is useless for locating fodder fish. On the deeper Waveney and Yare, however, it comes into its own because it can read depths and reveal worthwhile features such as drop-offs and holes. Few anglers use side-scan, but I have found it particularly useful when trolling and, while being far from a hundred per cent reliable, it has occasionally pinpointed pike holding up close to the bank. Subsequently, by working my baits hard up against the bank, I have been able to catch a few extra fish to over 25lb.

From the bank there is a public right to fish only where there is a public right of access. Many banks are privately owned, however, and others are remote and it is difficult to get access to the water from them. Fishing from a boat resolves these problems and is in keeping with the age-old rights granted by Magna Carta, that there is a public right to fish all tidal water by boat. However, this does not mean that you can go anywhere without restraint: the issue of tidal access requires legal interpretation and over the years the total or partial closure of certain Broads has occurred. As a legal challenge to a landowner's rights would be extremely procrastinated and expensive, it is highly unlikely that this will happen. The Broads Authority tends to favour the alternative approach of consultation and compromise by all concerned. While this is workable to some extent, there are still many Broads, particularly on the Bure, where this has not happened and where anglers have precious little access.

With the right of tidal access now being in such a mess, a number of pike anglers have adopted a poacher's charter and fish wherever they want. However, with many of the Broads being internationally important nature reserves, English Nature and the Broads Authority threaten poachers with legal action for deliberately disturbing a Site of Special Scientific Interest, the maximum fine being £20,000. If I have one overriding criticism of this action, it is that the same authorities have been slow to promote access to the Broads where wildlife protection is of less importance.

A Tour of the Broads

Having got our boat and being aware of the issues of access, let us now take a brief tour of the Broads. In the centre of Beccles, a pretty rural town on the banks of the River Waveney, which divides the two counties of Norfolk and Suffolk, there is a sign proclaiming Beccles to be the 'Beginning of the Broads'. I suppose Norwich could put up a similar sign in its city centre, but without doubt it is Wroxham on the Bure that really has the right to erect such a sign since it is the hub of the Broads' boating fleets.

The tidal Bure starts a few miles upstream of Wroxham in the village of Coltishall. From there downstream to Horning, the river mostly flows between heavily wooded banks, after which it becomes increasingly tidal and the Broadland landscape gradually more typically open. Pike can be caught anywhere along the river and I have even taken fish to 29lb 10oz from its tiny, non-navigable reaches far upstream of Coltishall Mill. In winter though, most pike tend to congregate into relatively short areas of river encompassing the two villages of Wroxham and Horning. This distribution of fish starts as the autumn sets in, brought about partly by salt tides pushing them out of the lower reaches and also by the concentrations of fodder fish that migrate into the large network of boatyards and dykes to overwinter in the comparative shelter there. Each winter this phenomenon occurs to various degrees on all the Broads river systems, although fishing pressure and salt surges can conspire to push fish out.

Throughout Wroxham and Horning the river is seldom more than around 6ft deep, with its flow being typically placid. It has become thick with roach in recent years and, not surprisingly, it produces lots of good doubles, although pike weighing much over 20lb are not abundant. Even so, most seasons the odd high 20 turns up, though 30s are rare.

Starting at Wroxham and working downstream, the Bure Broads that are officially accessible for angling include Wroxham Bridge Broad, Wroxham Broad, Salthouse Broad and

Chris Turnbull's 29lb 10oz lump, caught from the non-tidal Bure on a sardine.

Decoy Broad (Norwich and District members only). Then, downstream of Horning at the end of Ranworth Dyke, lies Maltby Broad (also known as Ranworth Outer Broad), and then finally we come to Fleet Dyke, which leads into South Walsham Outer Broad. A few pike can be found on any of the Broads throughout the winter, although sport is rarely hectic.

Flowing into the Bure at Ant Mouth just above St Bennet's Abbey, the River Ant is the only Broadland river that directly feeds into a Broad. While not generally as highly rated as the other rivers, it can be prolific, especially in its upper reaches around the Wayford Bridge and Hunset Mill area and also the boatyards around Sutton and Stalham. Most pike here are fairly small, although the odd fish over 20lb turns up. Downstream of these areas Barton Broad is a huge sheet of water covering 150 acres. Having recently been mud-pumped as part of a hugely ambitious restoration project, it is still available for angling and, while generally inconsistent, it manages to produce numbers of decent pike each season. That the Ant is capable of producing the occasional big pike I have no doubt, having once

been shown a photograph of a very big fish found dead after particularly bad salt-tides.

The River Thurne is, without doubt, the jewel in the crown of Broadland. Flowing into the lower Bure at Thurne Mouth a few miles downstream of the Ant's confluence, some may be surprised to learn that the Thurne is only 5 miles long. Its small size is surpassed by its huge reputation, as this legendary river has produced more big pike than any other river in the United Kingdom. Its reputation is enhanced considerably by the presence of Hickling Broad, Heigham Sound and Horsey Mere, three large, shallow, weedy broads, which collectively cover over 800 acres. I should also mention the three long navigation dykes that interconnect them – Deep Dyke, which leads from Heigham Sound to Hickling, Meadow Dyke, which leads from Heigham Sound to Horsey, and Candle Dyke, which joins this entire network to the Thurne. Near the village of Somerton lie the clear, weedy waters of Martham North and South Broads, environments which represent the natural, pristine condition of the Broads as they all were before the ravages of recent times.

A 25lb 1oz Heigham Sound chunk for Chris Turnbull; it took a mackerel head.

Chris Turnbull with a beautifully marked, Hickling 26lb 1oz, caught on a half mackerel.

Steve Last with a 27lb Heigham Sound specimen.

With the exception of Martham South Broad, all the Thurne Broads are available for fishing within certain constraints. For example, on Hickling and Duck Broad (part of Heigham Sound) certain important wildfowl refuge areas exist which, after 1 November, become voluntary no-go zones. Meanwhile, Martham South Broad is cosseted and locked away from the world by the Norfolk Wildlife Trust, although on the North Broad they run a strict permit system each winter. Finally, Horsey Mere is closed for fishing between 1 November and 1 March each winter.

The entire upper Thurne is once again going through a period of recovery following the *Prymnesium* blooms of 2000/01. It is an incredibly buoyant system that exists on a cruel knife-edge but, given time, perhaps it will return to its former glory. Without doubt, the large sizes its pike repeatedly achieve are in part down to the high mortality rates that regularly thin their numbers. It is a system that has numerous high and low periods, and this latest low will not be its last.

Downstream of Thurne Mouth, lost in the Bure marshes, Muck Fleet is effectively nothing more than a drainage dyke that runs into the Bure via a sluice. While quite unremarkable in itself, Muck Fleet flows out of a group of interconnected waters known as the Trinity Broads and consisting of Filby Broad, Eel's Foot (or Great Ormesby) Broad, Rollesby Broad, Lily Broad and Sportsman's (or Little Ormesby) Broad. Together, these waters also cover over 800 acres and perhaps offer the most easily accessible Broads pike-fishing experience, with dinghies being available for hire. There is also some bank fishing available where the roads transverse these Broads. Pike fishing is good too, with plenty of doubles and the odd 20 to be caught. While the top weight seldom exceeds around 27lb, every now and then a 30 is reported.

Now let us move on to the River Yare and its Broads. From the point where the River Wensum flows through the sluices at New Mills Yard, just north west of Norwich city centre, it becomes a tidal river that feeds into the Broads. On the south-east outskirts of the city, the little

Yare similarly flows through the last of its mill sluices at Trowse before draining into the considerably larger Wensum, where the Yare's name unjustly takes precedence.

Although the river bed is polluted with mercury and overrun with non-indigenous Asiatic clams, the Yare is very much an improved fishery in terms of its roach and bream stocks and hence pike. Twenty years ago 20s were virtually unheard of, although it had a reputation of being a prolific doubles fishery, particularly in Rockland and Surlingham Broads, which are situated close to Brundall village. Today, while the numbers of pike in the vicinity of Norwich and Brundall appear to be thinning, due no doubt to the amount of fishing pressure, their average size has greatly increased with specimens over 20lb being fairly common and the odd 30 showing up in most winters. Pike can also be caught far downstream of Brundall, but this soon becomes a remote area that is increasingly deep and formidable. Not surprisingly, these seldom-fished reaches could throw up the odd surprise.

Last, but certainly not least, we come to the River Waveney, the most southerly of the Broads rivers. At Geldeston Lock it is tidal and navigable but still has the genial charm of a gentle, upper river. By the time it reaches Beccles, however, it becomes strongly tidal with depths often exceeding 12ft. Indeed, by the time one travels downstream to the entrance of Oulton Dyke, which eventually joins it to Oulton Broad, it is no place for fools to go afloat without being professionally equipped. Without doubt, the Waveney offers prolific pike fishing at times, but it must be said that it is often moody and also prone to colour up after any amount of winter rain. While essentially a good doubles water, there are a number of decent 20s if you can find them, and every now and then it turns up a 30. Unfortunately, the 37lb fish that I was supposed to have caught there a few years ago was nothing more than a rumour. Oulton Broad itself is a large sheet of water in excess of 100 acres in area. Situated in the suburbs of Lowestoft, it is no oil painting although it is an excellent winter pike fishery that in recent years has produced pike over 30lb.

Methods and Techniques

Having provided a sketch of the Broads, let us turn to fishing them. My approach is fairly conventional although I have incorporated tips learned from many anglers I have fished with over the years.

Except when deadbait wobbling, which is a method I use with success, I always use floats when boat fishing, whether it be free roaming and paternostered livebaits or float-ledgered deadbaits. Achieving an effective bite indication from the bank is easy, but, when afloat, the boat is likely to be swaying, thus moving the floats all the time so that when a run occurs it is not always obvious. Because of this, particularly when deadbaiting during the autumn period when pike tend to wolf down the baits quickly, it is possible to experience a worrying percentage of fairly deeply hooked fish. While it is normally a simple operation to remove the hooks, this entails a bit of messing about that I would rather avoid. The best way to minimize deep hooking is to set the depth of the float at no more than 1ft or so overdepth and strike at the first indication.

Many boat anglers use loaded pencil floats for deadbaiting, but my own preference is for a round cork or poly-ball float painted black on the bottom half and Day-Glo orange on the top. While on the face of it such a float may seem crude, in practice I have found that, while the swaying of the boat keeps pulling pencil floats under, giving endless false indications, a corkball stays on the surface. Then, when a fish moves away with the bait, indication is normally heard via the loosely set baitrunner, while the float slides away over the surface. The same usually occurs when a run moves to the left or the right. These indications are generally not too difficult to see. But, when a pike runs slowly towards you, indication can be very poor with a loaded pencil float, whereas with a cork-ball the float will instantly change colour by showing you its black bottom as it moves towards you.

There are few deadbaits, both coarse and sea, that I have not succeeded in catching Broads pike on, but nothing beats mackerels and eels. I am

Chris Turnbull preparing to work a roach livebait over the top of weedbeds.

not talking about eel sections either but whole ones, which I generally air-inject at the head end and anchor down at the tail to make them sit up and beg. The trebles are set no more than 3in apart and hooked into the end of the tail. Perhaps surprisingly, runs are seldom missed.

The traditional, free-roaming livebait technique using a greased line and small, cigar-type float, will need no introduction and the same applies to paternosters, so all I shall say is that both methods are effective. I would make the point, though, that, when using a sunken float from a boat, effective bite indication is impossible and so I do not do it.

I usually employ a number of different methods when anchored up in a boat and it is entirely possible, with a little organizing, for two anglers to use three or four rods where appropriate. For myself, the best thing about boat fishing is that it

allows me to move frequently and to cover plenty of water. As pike often group up in what tend to be transient hotspots, runs tend to come fairly quickly when you locate them. Most areas are worth giving at least an hour without a run and, should I encounter some action, I am generally prepared to give an area up to an hour after each run. I tend to prefer to keep searching water rather than patiently waiting for the pike to search out my baits. I therefore reposition my deadbaits frequently and regularly twitch them back towards the boat. As a general rule, Broads pike tend to respond better to livebaits in high-barometric conditions with cold, clear water, with more action coming to deadbaits during low-pressure periods, with its usual coloured water and windy conditions. Another point to note is that, when on the Thurne Broads, I am entirely happy to restrict myself to deadbaits when out on their open flats, whereas when on the rivers the reverse is the case and I generally find livebaits to be far more effective.

It is not really possible to fish effectively with more than two anglers in a boat. Boat etiquette is something every angler has to work out with his fishing partner, but without it it is possible to sour friendships. Most experienced boat partners tend to anchor up in a position that allows them equal access to the area of water they are stationed in. By dividing the swim equally, with all the water off the front half of the boat belonging to one angler and all that off the back half belonging to the other, you can allow each other a fair bash at equal amounts of water. By using this approach you can anchor the boat up in a position parallel to the marginal reed fringe, thus providing each angler with the same opportunity to position baits alongside the reed fringe on one side of the boat, and also equal access to the open water on the other side. In strong winds, however, it can be easier to anchor the boat pointing into the wind and divide the boat so you fish off one side each. You want to avoid the bloke in the front from struggling to cast his rigs up into the wind while his mate effortlessly covers all the water downwind.

If, like me, your favourite trick is to position baits quickly, smack, bang along the halfway mark at right angles to the boat, thus squeezing your mate into a reduced area, then you must hope that he has a sense of humour. I remember

A 25lb 3oz River Thurne 'croc' for Chris Turnbull; it fell to a free-roamed livebait.

doing this to an old fishing partner John Sadd when we were anchored out in the middle of Heigham Sound. After I had sent a mackerel tail 60yd downwind, straight down the halfway mark, John gave me a sideways glance and then whacked a whole mackerel straight down the same line, dropping it 10yd beyond my float. There then followed a 10min stand-off, where we both waited to see who would give in and reposition his bait. As usual, John had all the sandwiches and so eventually, after twitching back my bait a couple of times, I relented and reeled in. Ten minutes later the baitrunner on John's rod burst into 'run music' and after a fairly energetic fight he had a fabulous, 29lb 12oz fish that really should have been mine!

I also recall that John tucked me up again on the penultimate day of the same season while we were anchored up on the west side of Horsey, near Waxham Cut, during gale-force winds that seemingly prevented anyone else venturing out on the water. John had been fishing Horsey for several days with nothing to show for his efforts. I had fished there a couple of days when the Broad had reopened on 1 March and taken a double or two but had since concentrated my efforts on the top end of the main river. I had arranged to accompany John for the last day or two of the season. With his dinghy *Snagglepuss* chained up overnight in the windmill dyke on the east side of Horsey, we had little option but to cross the Broad in the teeth of the wind, with the outboard flat out. Possibly we were mad, certainly we were obsessed! The last time I had done this I had been soaked by the spray as I throttled the outboard and steered the boat into the rolling, white-capped waves, while my mate Jim hung on tightly at the front of the boat. Having not zipped up my one-piece suit, the first few waves of spray flew over Jim's head and hit me full in the face and chest before pouring down inside my one-piece. I spent the rest of that day with my naughty bits tucked into a thermal mitten to keep them warm. I took a 20 though, so I had no reason to complain.

But this time, as I steered the boat out into the rolling white caps, I gritted my teeth and made sure that I was properly zipped up, while John shrank down inside his waterproofs at the other end of the boat. Eventually, having worked our way across the open Broad, we dropped the mud-weights in the lea of the marginal reed fringe, before bailing out the boat, tidying up the mayhem and eventually casting our baits out in a wide arc. While these conditions are hard work to be out in, Broads pike love a good blow on the water so that, even though Horsey had been hard work all week, I was feeling really confident. I said as much to John and, while he agreed, I suspected that he was long past expecting any action. Here, in the shelter of the tall reeds, we were spared from the worst of the wind-chill and, while John tucked into the first of his sandwiches, I stood in the back of the boat looking out over the waves in eager anticipation.

I find such conditions exhilarating and, following a rather stupid practice that a few of my mates and I used to share to pass the day, I broke out into a loud and tuneless, improvised song. It was all about how I was going to give John a much deserved piking lesson. He looked at me doubtingly while trying to dream up a suitable verse as a retort. Pushing my luck further, I started a new line about how a pike was just about to pick up my bait, but, no sooner had the words passed my lips, than I noticed that one of my floats had started moving sideways through the waves. He had not noticed, so, breaking into the next verse, I started singing about how my reel was just about to burst into run-music and, precisely on cue, my baitrunner started to accompany me. John looked at me incredulously and continued to do so as I wound down and set the hooks. By the time I had reeled the fish the 70yd or so to the boat, he had eventually accepted that it was not just a wind up. That fish may have weighed only 15lb, but it was worth its weight in gold. The problem though is that my story does not end there .... Within a few minutes of returning my fish, another baitrunner burst into song, but this time it was John's. After five long minutes of huffing and puffing he finally drew a somewhat bigger fish over the waiting net. As we rolled her out on the underlay, it was evident that this fish was going to be very close to the magic mark. On the scales she went 30lb 10oz and the rest of that day it was John who did all the singing! It turned out later, after comparing the photographs, that this fish was the same one as he had caught at 29lb 12oz from Heigham Sound back in December, which, if nothing else, proves how migratory Thurne pike can be.

Livebait trolling is another traditional Broads technique I have found incredibly effective, provided that windy conditions do not make boat control impossible. Trolling can efficiently search a lot of water, even when done at very low speeds, which is how I find it the most effective. Occasionally, it is possible to cover miles of water with very little action, but it is rare not to

locate eventually a few fish that could easily be missed by using more static methods. I normally follow a policy of either trolling the rivers or otherwise grid-searching the Broads by anchoring up for an hour or so in several promising areas and covering them with a variety of baits. Trolling can nevertheless be equally effective out on the flats, provided that the weed is not too high in the water. Having caught a fish or two in one area while trolling, it is often tempting to drop the mud-weights and put out static baits or free-roamers. Sometimes this will pick up fish but often it does not, then, as soon as you lift the mud-weights and start trolling again, takes occur almost instantly as the boat goes over their heads. What I think happens is that

Pete Garvan with that rarest of creatures – a Bure 30.

the boat actually stirs otherwise torpid fish into motion, having the effect of kick-starting them into striking at a bait as it follows the boat through the swim.

For trolling, biggish baits and plenty of weight to keep them down in the water are real advantages. I have heard it said that trolling is not a particularly good method for catching big pike, but having taken lots of mid 20s when trolling I cannot see any truth in this notion.

Here I am reminded of an occasion when another friend gave me a whopping. This time it was in December 1987. Pete Garvan had come up from London to visit for a few days in order to do a slideshow for the Norfolk Anglers Conservation Association, following which we had planned couple of days on the Bure at Horning. At that time, I had only recently got to grips with trolling and had been enjoying some first-class fishing there. Two to five doubles a day were the norm along with numbers of smaller fish but I was still to pick up a 20.

After his slideshow, we launched the dinghy at dawn from the bank at Horning Ferry and set about searching the river. The conditions were ideal for trolling – clear water and a gentle breeze. We worked my hotspot area outside the boatyards, but a single jack each was all we had for our efforts. After searching the river throughout the village and for a considerable distance upstream, it was obvious that few fish were present, so halfway through the afternoon we decided to return to the boatyard area and work it thoroughly for the rest of the day. This turned out to be a good idea as I soon caught a low double, which was eventually followed up with my first Horning 20 – 23lb 10oz. Pete struggled and, if I was starting to feel a bit smug after catching a few fish, I was trying not to show it. Anyway, he had tossed his baits over the back of the boat while we were dealing with my 20 and, as I was still unhooking it, he suddenly let out a yelp that his float had gone. After quickly winding down he bent into what was obviously a good fish. As soon as we had lifted it into the

boat our knees started knocking as we quickly came to terms with how big it was. On the scales she weighed 30lb 1oz, which is a real monster for the Bure. You cannot imagine his delight, although, believe it or not, he has never been back to fish Norfolk. But I guess when your one and only double from the Broads weighs over 30lb there is little need to push your luck.

As for myself, I went on to take the trolling method to the shallow weedy reaches of the River Thurne and took the place apart before others eventually cottoned on and followed my lead. I then turned my attention to the deserted expanses of Hickling Broad, until that also eventually became too busy. Today, my fishing has moved on again and, while I still fish the Broads from time to time, I am no longer obsessed as I used to be. Maybe that flame will be rekindled one day, but at the moment I am happy with my memories. I never caught that Thurne 30 that haunted my dreams though, despite catching a good number of fish over 25lb.

Finally then, what does the future hold for the Broads more generally? Set against the spiral of general ecological degradation, it is difficult to envisage a new golden age of Broads piking. Such is the state of modern pike fishing that misinformation is necessarily part and parcel of protecting one's fishing so, not surprisingly, many 'outsiders' assume that local anglers paint a gloomy picture of the state of their fishing to put others off from coming. While obviously this does happen, the fact is that, as good as Broads pike fishing might be compared to many parts of the country, it is certainly not as good as it was. In particular, while pike over 30lb are caught every year, any angler setting his sights on building up a tally of 30s would be better off adopting the modern bounty-hunter approach of targeting known big fish around the country or staying on the trout reservoir circuit. The main charm of the Broads is that it is still possible to get away from the crowds in a few areas and, for any angler who simply wants to indulge in some diverse and interesting pike fishing, the area still has much to offer.

3 FENLAND PIKE FISHING

Dick Culpin

'It had been a very long day. He had been on the water since before dawn and now, as twilight approached, he began to think that his only reward was going to be the two jacks that he had caught first thing that morning. Having walked over 2 miles with a rucksack, cool bag, livebait bucket and three rods, he was tired and beginning to think about the long drive home. He reckoned that, at best, there was another 15min of light and decided on one last move before calling it a day.

'With the baits cast and strategically placed in the drain he stood motionless, with the fresh easterly wind in his face. One thing was for certain – he would have a very healthy glow about him when he got home. Then it happened. One of his bright orange floats seemed to shiver before bobbing and moving purposely across the drain, slowly sinking as it went. He was quickly on to the rod and, having seen that the line was gently peeling off the reel, he re-engaged the bail arm and struck. The resistance he felt immediately confirmed that, unlike the fish that he had caught earlier in the day, this was likely to be a much bigger proposition. The line was singing in the wind and he was making very little progress as the pike, as yet unseen, doggedly made its bid for freedom. The light was now quickly disappearing and he was experiencing difficulty in seeing exactly where the fish was. But, with patience, care and years of experience, he slowly but surely was gaining the upper hand and eventually he sunk his net and drew what was clearly a very large pike into the welcoming mesh.

'A sigh of relief was quickly followed by the warm inner feeling that signals any achievement. The only sound was the wind. The formality of unhooking was quickly completed and

his mind turned to the weight of his capture. The pike was safely enclosed in his giant weigh sling and he gently lifted her on to the scales. The dial indicated a weight of just over 25lb. He gently lowered the fish and went through the weighing process again to confirm a weight of 25lb 3oz. He punched the air and shouted aloud, his efforts had been rewarded.

'Two quick photographs in the half light were quickly followed by his gently lowering her back into the dark still-waters of this Fenland drain. A matter of seconds passed before she pulled away from his guiding hand and slid out of sight to become nothing more than a magnificent memory.'

This account provides a flavour of the pike-fishing possibilities in Fenland, a windswept area of low, flat land lying south of The Wash. It comprises most of Cambridgeshire, but also includes parts of southern Lincolnshire, the

A personal best for Dick Culpin from the Fens – 25lb 2oz.

Dick Culpin with a fine 22lb 12oz drain-caught pike.

west of Norfolk and the edge of Suffolk. The centre is Ely, meaning Eel Island, with eels and fish in general being part of the livelihood of the old 'fenmen' when the area consisted of largely marshland, until it was drained for agricultural use in the middle of the seventeenth century. Today it is an area of excellent agricultural land with more recent drains, including the Relief Channel, having been constructed in the 1960s. It was around that time that anglers such as Ray Webb, Barrie Rickards, Bill Chillingsworth and Hugh Reynolds starting catching some excellent pike and, although there have been some less prolific periods since, good pike fishing is still to be had.

Fenland includes rivers such as the Nene and the Great Ouse together with a maze of drains. The rivers, unlike in their upper reaches, are largely deep and slow flowing in the open Fen

countryside. The drains are straight and equally slow-flowing channels with the water levels controlled by pumps. Perhaps the most famous ones are the Twenty Foot, the Sixteen Foot, the Forty Foot and the Hundred Foot, together with the Old River Nene, the Middle Level Main Drain and the Relief Channel itself. Most of these waters are often thought of as being rather boring and featureless, this making it difficult for pike anglers new to the area to know where to start. As the reader will be only too well aware, you have to know where the pike are likely to be in order to catch them and so in what follows I begin by locating pike on such waters. I then look at some of the main methods of catching them by focusing on livebaiting, deadbaiting and lure fishing. Apart from wanting to catch pike though, there are other reasons why many of us enjoy our fishing. It is also, for instance, about relaxing, being out in the countryside, often with good friends, where amusing incidents take place. I give examples of this, what might be called the lighter side of pike fishing. Finally, despite some concerns about increased angling pressure such as the renewed catching of pike for the pot, I end on an optimistic note as far as fishing in Fenland is concerned.

Location, Location, Location

Unlike Tony Blair's old and broken promise to the electorate that he would concentrate on education, I can promise the reader that location, location, location is the key to success when pike fishing in the Fens. Not least this is because, as I mentioned, at first glance many of the rivers and drains appear boring and featureless. Over the years anglers who are better qualified than I have written extensively about the need to work out where the pike are going to be. It must be emphasized, however, that there are no short cuts and the only way to reap any reward eventually is through hard work.

A good way to start is to invest in the Ordnance Survey (OS) maps that cover the Fens and these are mainly OS Maps 142, 143 and 153. When scanning them it will quickly become evident that there is a lot of water, which in itself may be a daunting prospect to anglers new to the area. Closer inspection, however, will inevitably give pointers, not least of which will be access points and potential features that may be worth exploring. As far as access is concerned, many rivers and drains are on farmland and it is certainly not acceptable to drive up private roads and park without permission. Most farmers are accommodating individuals who would probably not have too much of a problem giving permission, provided that you ask first rather than after the event. I have known circumstances where anglers have returned to their car only to find that its tyres had been let down or that strongly worded notices had been stuck on the windscreen. My advice then is to ask first.

The OS maps will clearly show features on rivers and drains, including bridges, bends, electricity pylons, pumping stations and ditches, side drains and tributaries. All of these are worth

The River Cam in winter.

Another drain-caught pike of 22lb 6oz for Dick Culpin.

investigating and it may be best to do so before fishing. Indeed, I cannot offer any better advice than that provided by that great Fen angler, the previously mentioned Bill Chillingworth, who suggested that, ideally, you should explore these waters at dawn or at dusk. By doing so you are likely to find evidence of prey fish, such as surface topping, which usually means that the pike will not be far away. As to the features themselves, they certainly warrant further comment.

Beginning with bridges, any manmade structure on a river or a drain has the potential to attract prey fish and therefore predators. In particular, perch are often found lurking around the structure that makes up a bridge, having been attracted by the shoals of fish such as roach, bleak and minnows that gather there. There is no doubt that pike will be attracted to such areas as they prey on the perch themselves as well as the other shoal fish.

As for bends, while many of the drains that you will come across have few, if you do happen to find an area where there is a slight deviation from a straight line, it is well worth exploring. They are more frequently found on the main rivers which, apart from those mentioned earlier, include the Cam, the Lark, the Wissey and the Little Ouse. Not all bends will produce something, but again an early morning or late evening investigation of these areas will quickly tell the angler whether prey fish are present and therefore the likelihood of pike being found. The actual fishing of bends is very much an individual's choice, but it is probably worth saying that, while the near shelf and the far shelf are well worth exploring, this does not mean that the middle of the drain or river should be neglected.

The flow, particularly of the rivers, will inevitably have the effect of either silting up or gouging out shelves and a bait strategically placed in the drop-off zone has a very good chance of being found by a pike.

Across the Fens there is a massive network of electricity pylons, which inevitably transverse the rivers and drains. It goes without saying that these areas are potentially dangerous to anglers, particularly the match boys with their roach poles, but there is little doubt that the area in close proximity to a pylon could be described as a feature. The main reason for this is that many of the rivers and drains are dredged from time to time. Inevitably dredging operations around an area where pylons cross a river or a drain are limited because a dredger would not be able to operate safely under the area where the pylons cross the water. This can result in there being a small plateau in the area immediately beneath the pylon, with the consequence that there will be a slight drop-off on either side where the dredging has been completed. This is a natural holding area for prey fish and therefore pike.

The areas around pumping stations will often attract prey fish and the pike will not be far behind. However, the area very close to a station is not always productive since quite often the pike will actually hold up some distance away. It almost seems that that area is the pike's larder and they merely move into that area when it is time to feed. By definition, therefore, they spend a great deal more time nearby rather than actually in the feeding zone so that to introduce baits into the holding area is always likely to lead to success.

Many of the waters that we encounter in the Fens will have tributaries running into them by the way of smaller drains and ditches. While not every area like this will produce they are certainly worth investigation and one way of doing this is by fishing them with lures in the summer months. Again, to study local OS maps will help considerably since many of the side drains and ditches will be easily identifiable, thus saving valuable time and energy in physically looking for them.

Methods

Moving to methods, there is little doubt that all the usual ones work in the Fens, which should not come as a real surprise. Beginning with live-baits, in the Fens we have exactly the same problems as other areas of the country. There are those who are for them and those against. Consequently, like elsewhere, there are some waters where livebaiting is strictly prohibited and others where it is allowed. It is important therefore to observe the local rules and regulations with regard to this issue.

Whatever the pros and cons, the use of live-bait has always been a method that has enjoyed great success in Fenland. Many anglers practise this method week in and week out, taking good fish into the bargain. However, as in many waters, the method often produces small pike even when the livebait itself is of a reasonable size. Many anglers give up a lot of pike fishing time to catch livebaits and I am sure that they are disappointed when, despite all their hard work, the majority of their subsequent runs lead to small pike being landed. That is not to say that the livebaits will not produce big pike, as they frequently do, but on a lot of waters it is a question of wading through the jacks before eventually connecting with a half-decent-sized fish. You also have to bear in mind that, in many areas, not only are you likely to attract pike but zander will not be far behind, though many of us do not regard this as a bad thing.

As for the types of bait, there has been much written about the fact that, if you locate the bream shoals in Fenland waters, you will quickly come across the pike. Bream do make good baits and small skimmers up to 1lb in weight will work well on most waters. However, in my view, although bream and all the usual coarse suspects work well, roach probably top the list, followed perhaps by rudd. These two species are plentiful throughout the Fens and, generally speaking, they are reasonably easy to catch except in the hardest of winters. Incidentally, roach are not just the most popular bait for pike but also again for zander. Other good baits that work well for pike are trout, perch and chub. Perch and chub are reasonably easy to catch on the main rivers, particularly the Cam and the Granta.

A method that has consistently produced a great deal of fish is float-paternostered lives, particularly on the major rivers such as the Great Ouse, the Cam and the Lark. Placing such a bait on the outside of a deep bend, for example, or alongside an overhanging tree or bush (even though sometimes they can be few and far between in Fenland) can often bring success.

Many drains are very narrow yet still hold good heads of pike. The presentation of a live-bait in these circumstances can be difficult and certainly the use of a free-roving bait can be awkward. In these circumstances there are anglers who are happy to employ the method first used by Dennis Pye in the late 1950s and the early 1960s, namely the use of the dumb-bell float. This comprises two connected spheres fished as a slider. It provides extra resistance, thereby enabling you to control the bait in a tight swim, and this can be important. There is no doubt that this has put a great deal of fish on the bank for those that have perfected the art, examples being Derrick Amies and my own mate Denis Moules.

The Great Ouse when it really blew!

I have already mentioned the use of trout and would encourage the use of paternoster tactics when using these baits, since a free rover can often outpace a pike. Ledgered livebaits certainly do work, but a great deal of attention has to be given to bite indication to prevent deep hooked fish or even bite-offs.

But despite the success that livebaits can bring – at least in terms of numbers as opposed to size of pike – it is probably fair to say that deadbaits are the most common method employed in the Fens, and these can be fished in a number of ways. The trusty method of either ledgered or float-ledgered deadbaits will consistently bring results on any of the waters. A method that seems to have been neglected though, particularly in recent years as lures have become the vogue, is that of deadbait wobbling.

I recently met a small group of anglers on the River Delph at Welney and each was armed with a single rod, a bag of deadbait, a landing net and that was about it. They passed the time of day with me as I was sitting there drowning three static deadbaits. Some three hours later they returned on their way to the Lamb and Flag pub for a pint at lunchtime. Having enquired as to their success, they told me that they had taken fourteen fish, five of which were doubles with the biggest being just under 18lb. The methods they employed were very simple, being sink-and-draw wobbled baits cast across the river to the overhanging trees, with the bait being worked back across the water, with takes often occurring in the middle of the river. There is no doubt that this small band had identified a method that worked particularly well on this river and at that time of the year (autumn). Perhaps there is a lesson there for all of us.

A method I have employed, much to the dismay of some of my fellow pikers, is the use of paternostered deadbaits. I am not sure why they seem to look down at such a technique because it must be said that this has worked particularly well for me, especially when rivers such as the Ouse and the Cam have got a fairly heavy flow. My view is that the flow of the river works the deadbait so as to make it rise and fall,

albeit only a few inches, thus making it an attractive proposition to a pike that probably views the bait as a fish that is very close to death. I have caught a number of 20lb-plus pike by employing this method.

The choice of bait, wherever you fish, is very much a personal thing and experimentation is likely to bring its own rewards. The baits that I have tinkered with, and to some degree have had success with, include whiting, sprats, red snapper and kippers. However, if I had to choose one deadbait to use when fishing in the Fens there is no doubt that it would have to be lamprey. Whether you use the fish whole or cut in half, there is no question that its bloody qualities are irresistible to the pike. There have also been numbers of zander into double figures caught on what is, in my view, an exceptional bait. All that said, the reader must not run away with the idea that lamprey is the only successful deadbait. Nothing could be further from the truth since sea baits such as herring, mackerel and sardine have all also worked well.

At this stage it is probably worth talking about water clarity (or otherwise). Anyone who regularly fishes the Fens will be aware that water conditions vary greatly from area to area. For example, the Great Ouse generally has good clarity, except in severe flood conditions, whereas the Lark that flows into the Great Ouse north of Ely is almost always coloured. Similarly, you will come across land drains where the colour can be really off putting and you even begin to doubt whether there are any pike in them. Such areas, however, should not be neglected since pike do inhabit these waters and will feed even in conditions that might be better suited to barbel or chub fishing. What is more, as a general rule I would tend to use a smelly deadbait in such conditions, with mackerel, herring and, of course, lamprey probably topping the list.

Coarse deadbaits will all have their day and inevitably from time to time they will attract zander. If the reader decides to target zander, the best advice that can be offered is that the baits used should be as fresh as possible. A roach that has been in the freezer for three months is unlikely to prove particularly appetizing as far as a zander is concerned. A pike, however, is less discerning and is likely to pick up a bait that might be described as less than fresh.

Another bait that has enjoyed great success is an eel section. It is also my belief that eels somehow attract larger pike and, in my experience, I can honestly say that I have never caught a jack on eel section. In addition, it is worth emphasizing a couple of tips that I have picked up concerning the use of eel baits. First, if you happen to be fishing for eels to use as bait, rather than kill them on the bank side you would be better served keeping them alive, transporting them home in a suitably tied carrier bag and then dropping them into the freezer. This will obviously have the effect of killing the eel but the beauty is that all the slime is retained, which is unquestionably very attractive as far as pike are concerned. You should then allow them to defrost sufficiently for them to be cut into appropriate bait-size sections and returned to the freezer for use at a later date. Secondly, whenever I use eel section I use a pair of scissors and forceps to cut away a section of the skin in order to mount the hooks. The eel does have a tough skin and before I used to do this I had a number of runs where I did not connect with the fish simply because the hooks did not pull free from the bait. By slotting the hooks into the cut, fleshy part of the bait, rather than into its skin, this problem seems to have been overcome. Moreover, it also is a well-known fact that eels are used as livebaits for catfish on the continent and my understanding is that, to prevent tangling, their tails are cut off before they are used. I have never tried this when pike fishing and equally I do not know of anyone who has, but it probably would lead to success.

Much has been written about buoyant baits and there is no doubt that popped-up deadbaits do work extremely well and it is certainly a method that should not be ignored when fishing in the Fens. What does concern me, however, is the use of polystyrene or other foreign bodies inside the deadbait. Working on the assumption that at least some of these baits would actually

The 'pike friendly' pop-up.

be swallowed by the pike, I am not convinced that we are doing them any favours by introducing alien materials into their food stock. My advice therefore is to employ a pop-up method where the pop-up itself is connected to the trace by means of a small section of wire so as to prevent bite-offs. In this way you can be rest assured that the pike will not swallow the buoyant material, added to which you will always get it back since the wire connection prevents bite-offs and the loss of the pop-up.

Over the years, the use of oil additives in deadbaits to enhance flavour has begun and there has also been a degree of experimentation with bait colouring. While oil additives can enhance deadbait flavours, in my experience there is often a danger of overdoing it. The oils available now are very concentrated and a misjudgement in the amount employed may actually have the effect of putting the fish off. I have similar misgivings about bait colouring. Many tackle shops have gone out of their way to provide deadbaits in a variety of colours, and although there is no doubt that these baits will catch pike, I remain to be convinced that coloration has actually got anything to do with success. It may be stating the obvious, but in my view a well-presented deadbait in the right place is the real key to success.

Dick Culpin and his personal best lure-caught pike – 18lb 10oz from the River Cam.

Let us now turn to lure fishing in the Fens. This is as popular here as it is elsewhere in the country, and there is no doubt that many anglers who regularly fish Fenland waters do use artificials with success. For example, even though my own experience of fishing with lures is somewhat limited, I have taken pike up to 18lb 10oz. In addition, it should be noted that within the membership of the Cambridge region of the Pike Anglers Club (PAC), a number of members devote much time to lure fishing. This is especially so in the spring and summer months and some of their catches have been spectacular. On occasions it is not unknown for as many as fifty pike being taken between two anglers in a single day. Inevitably many jacks are also caught, but there is always a possibility of picking up doubles and, indeed, larger fish.

Many of the rivers and drainage systems in the Fens are quite shallow and the use of surface lures and those that have a running action down to about 3ft will often produce. During the summer many of these waters are heavily weeded, which in itself should not be a deterrent to the determined lure angler. By using surface lures with weed guards, the sport can be fantastic, with explosive takes providing many heart-stopping moments.

As with other branches of our sport, often the best time to lure fish is at either dawn or dusk since the middle of the day sees the pike becoming lethargic and disinclined to feed. You will always get circumstances where the occasional fish will be picked up in the heat of the day, but generally an early morning or evening session will produce the goods.

Although this book is devoted to pike fishing, it would be wrong not to mention the fact that lures will also account for zander and perch. Both can be targeted and there have been several occasions when I have been lure fishing on stretches of the Cam when reasonable zander have been taken on spinnerbaits and spoons.

On some of the larger rivers, such as the Great Ouse and the Cam, trolling lures has proved to be very successful. This method covers a great deal of water and, although there can be periods of inactivity, equally it is possible to locate hotspots and take numbers of fish from a relatively small area. Under these circumstances it is advisable to stop trolling, anchor up and chuck a few lures around in the area where the takes have materialized. Once the action dries up it is merely a question of continuing the troll and finding another hotspot further along the river.

Another important point is that lure fishing in the summer months can often lead to the identification of areas that can subsequently be bait-fished in the colder months. There has been many an occasion where summer sorties with lures catching jacks have subsequently led to bigger fish being taken by more traditional methods in the winter months.

Despite the success that lures can bring, my only slight reservation in relation to using them is that hook sizes on some lures can harm the pike, either in the area of its mouth or of its eyes. Thus it is rare for me to use outsize lures with big hooks, except perhaps when fishing on reservoirs and the like. In the Fens there is probably no need to go over the top with the lure and hook size, with the result that injury to the pike is kept to a minimum.

Not Just the Pike Fishing

Although we all want to catch pike, this is not the only reason for being on and enjoying the rivers and drains of Fenland. Often it is simply about being out in the fresh air and the countryside. In addition, though, the Fens themselves provide an area blessed with all sorts of animal and bird life and so the patient and observant angler is likely to have his day enriched by their presence.

And so there are regular sightings of such as foxes, stoats, weasels, deer and the occasional water vole. Seeing these animals in their natural habitat is certainly something to behold. But like everywhere else, we do have our problem creatures, including mink and cormorants. While I recognize the damage that they can cause to our fish stocks, I would simply put into the mind of the reader that their presence in our waters is not their fault. The reality of the situation is that animal rights campaigners and activists have been responsible for mink being released into the countryside, while our plundering of fish stocks at sea has driven the cormorant inland.

As for bird life more generally, being a keen 'twitcher', I invariably have my binoculars with me when I am fishing. Regular sightings include several birds of prey, including barn owls, short-eared owls, hobbys, kestrels and sparrowhawks. Many other birds are seen, such as many species of waders, ducks, geese and the inevitable kingfisher. Additionally, areas around the Ouse Washes, for example, at Welches Dam, will give the angler ample opportunity to see whooper and Bewick swans during their annual migration from Russia. As a slight aside, although I do support the limited culling of cormorants, a balance is needed and we, as anglers, do need to respect the opinions of other bodies such as the Royal Society for the Protection of Birds.

In short then, to my mind you cannot really call yourself an angler unless you have an appreciation of the countryside and of the environment in which you are seeking enjoyment. The chance to experience such thrills as the sight of the ghostly, white barn owl silently flying over a field at daybreak or dusk is one to be savoured and should be an important part of any angler's day. In addition, as with the Norfolk Broads, the flatness of the Fenland landscape lends itself to big skies with wonderful sunrises and sunsets. All this surely adds to the enjoyment and anticipation that we all experience when we are looking for our old friend esox. Furthermore, the

The River Cam at sunset.

point has to be made that the countryside and the environment in which we enjoy our fishing is fragile. We need to look after it and the creatures in it. As an example, I am sure the majority of readers will not have a problem with taking their own litter home. But can I merely ask that, if you do come across somebody else's rubbish, rather than leaving it there and commenting on how disgusting other anglers or water users are, please take it home with you and dispose of it properly.

The Lighter Side

On a different tack, no matter what species you happen to target there is no doubt that most anglers will have experienced amusing incidents along the way. Pike fishing is certainly no different in this respect and I would like to share with you a few that have happened to me when fishing in the Fens.

Not so very long ago I had decided to take an afternoon off work in order to fish a section of the

Sixteen Foot Drain at March. I had spent the morning with a client of mine in March itself and, having finished our business around midday I headed off to the drain. In my job as an insurance broker there is a need for me to wear a suit and tie and therefore I had to get out of my work clothing into my fishing gear. Being a tidy sort of chap, I neatly laid out my suit and work shirt on the parcel shelf of my car, locked up and walked the short distance across the road that runs alongside the drain and set up for an afternoon session. Everything was going really well and I had taken three fish, including a couple of doubles when, around three o'clock, I was aware of someone standing on the bank behind me. I looked round to see a police officer with radio in hand. He asked me whether the car parked at the opposite junction was mine, which I confirmed, and asked if he needed me to move it. His

concern was not with my parking but, in his words, he thought he had a 'Reggie Perrin' on his hands. Having seen my suit neatly laid out on the parcel shelf, he was under the impression that he was having to deal with a suicide! To find that I was only fishing came as something of a relief to him, as I am sure that he was half-expecting to find a bloated body floating down the river. We both had a really good laugh about the matter before he radioed into his station to tell them that all was well and they did not need to bring out the body bags.

Another incident occurred more recently. Most pike anglers usually fish with a mate and I suspect that most of us hope that there will be opportunities to catch decent fish at the same time, thus providing the opportunity for a self-timed, team photograph. This happened to my mate Paul Conway and me when we were fishing

Self-timed photographs can go wrong – Dick Culpin with a 17lb 10oz and Paul Conway with a 20lb 7oz.

a small drain and simultaneously took fish of 17lb 10oz to me and Paul's first 20 at 20lb 7oz. Having unhooked both fish and weighed them, we secured them in retaining sacks while we set up the camera equipment. The moment had arrived for us to get a self-timed shot of the pair of us holding our prizes. However, once again sod's law kicked in and, just as we were smiling for the camera, Paul's fish bucked in his hand, resulting in, to say the least, a rather amusing photograph. We did nevertheless manage to get a decent shot once we had stopped laughing.

Finally, most of us will have read in the angling press articles about young kids catching big fish. A similar situation took place some years ago when I took a pal of mine, Gary, and his eleven-year-old son David pike fishing in the Fens for the first time. They finished up remaining in the same spot for the best part of four hours without a hint of a run. Young David decided to reel his rod in, probably for the umpteenth time, and the movement of the bait prompted a strike and, the next thing I knew, I was looking at him with an alarming bend in his rod. Gary shouted to me for assistance and, after what seemed like an age, David managed to bring what was clearly a very large pike to the net. The netting was achieved without any problem and the pike was presented to David in the hope of showing him how to handle the fish and take the hooks out. But, on seeing the size of its mouth and the teeth contained therein, he decided that, at least for the time being, it would be better to leave the handling to his dad and me. We duly sorted things out and the pike weighed just over 20lb and was far and away the biggest that we caught that day. To prove that this was no fluke, on the very next trip but on a different drain, David managed to land another great fish of just over 19lb. It would be great to say that he got on to bigger and better things, but, as with all the young, in later life he was led astray by the distractions of beer and women. At the moment I think it is fair to say that he is still concentrating on those pleasures.

While most pike anglers take their sport seriously, we should never lose sight of the fact that, at the end of the day, it is only fishing and that there are far more serious things to worry about in this world of ours. To be able to enjoy the company of a fellow angler and have a few laughs along the way is surely as important as the catching of the fish itself.

A Matter of Current Concern

Before concluding, if there is one major area of concern that does need to be addressed it is that of long-lining together with angling pressure from, and I do not want to sound xenophobic, people from the enlarged European Community coming into the Fens to seek employment. In particular, there has been a worrying trend of groups of such people being seen on the banks of our rivers and drain systems frequently taking numbers of pike, and, indeed, other species too for the pot. We, and by that I mean the PAC, are currently lobbying the Environment Agency about this in order to try to get the byelaws changed. We want to restrict the numbers of fish that can be taken and, more importantly, limitations on the size of fish that can be taken. In an ideal world, of course, we would prefer that no fish at all were taken. Whether we can achieve this and whether the Environment Agency can police the area in a way that will help is unlikely. The onus therefore is on all true pike anglers to be vigilant and not be afraid of challenging others when it is clear that our sport is being damaged. There will be absolutely no point in our bemoaning a decline in fishing if we ourselves are not prepared to do something about it. It also remains important for all anglers who fish the Fens, whether regularly or infrequently, to remain vigilant and, not least, treat all pike with care and consideration. The message is make sure that you really do care, and, having got this off my chest, I now want to end on a more positive note.

Anyone who has read anything about pike fishing in the Fens will undoubtedly come to the conclusion that the fishing was probably at its best in the late 1960s and throughout the 1970s. After that there was a period of some decline for several reasons, including pollution, bad angling

The next generation – Jack Culpin with a good pike.

practice and culling policies. Thankfully, due in no small part to the efforts of the PAC, over the last ten years or so the fishing in the Fens has enjoyed something of a resurgence and so the future is brighter for the next generation of anglers. This is not only true of the pike fishing but also of most aspects of coarse angling.

That said, the reader must not run away with the idea that merely by turning up he will latch into 20 and 30lb pike. You only have to read that excellent publication by Denis Moules, *The Fenland 30s* to realize that a 30lb fish is a rare beast indeed and that only a few privileged anglers have achieved this feat. Most of the main river systems and drains are capable of producing fish in the 20lb class but fish over 25lb must also be regarded as rarities. Double-figure fish are reasonably plentiful throughout the Fens and certainly members of the PAC Cambridge Region who are able to devote time to their pike fishing have regularly caught between fifty and a hundred doubles per season. I want to emphasize that success will be achieved only by hard work, experimentation and dedication. I would also suggest that it is difficult for a single angler to achieve success on his own since it is very much a team thing, with information being shared among a small band of dedicated anglers. Nevertheless, overall the Fens are in good shape and they certainly can provide some interesting and productive pike fishing.

4 SOME OF THE BIG PIKE WATERS IN THE MIDLANDS OF ENGLAND

Neville Fickling

Although I am a Norfolk man, fate has seen that much of my adult life has been spent on the edge of north Lincolnshire in a small town called Gainsborough. I never thought for one moment when passing through this nondescript place on a train journey to Manchester that I would ever end up living there. Although I yearned to be back in Norfolk, as it happened, I found myself positioned nicely to exploit some of the best pike fishing we have seen, namely Blithfield and Ladybower reservoirs. It also placed me near to a giant river, the Trent, whose potential for big pike has yet to be fully explored.

Before dealing with these three big pike waters of the Midlands, it must be pointed out that this area of England also has many other pike fishing opportunities. There are rivers, canals, reservoirs and gravel pits, drains and a host of lakes and ponds, which are available to the pike angler. For example, concerning rivers, the Severn and, as we shall see, the Trent are the main ones and both have good stocks of pike. The former rises in Wales before flowing through Shropshire, Hereford and Worcester on its way to the Bristol Channel. The latter begins in Staffordshire before flowing eastwards through Nottinghamshire to the Humber Estuary. And there are other good pike rivers such as the Witham in Lincolnshire and the Ancholme in south Humberside. When it comes to canal pike one has only to mention the Grand Union Canal, which stretches from Birmingham towards Northampton, but there are also many smaller ones including those that traverse the west Midlands around Birmingham. Reservoirs are legion and include ones such as the 46-acre Saddington Reservoir between Leicester and Market Harborough. And with regard to drains we have those in Lincolnshire,

such as the Sibsey Trader and Hobhole around Boston. All these waters and others too numerous to mention provide some excellent pike fishing. Unfortunately, space prevents me from elaborating on them here, not least because it is the three big pike waters mentioned earlier that I want to deal with in this chapter. So let us begin with Blithfield.

Blithfield Reservoir

In this country we are unusual in that many of our big water supply reservoirs have been developed as stocked trout waters. In any other country, such as France, a water supply reservoir would have been stocked with carp and would now be lined with little green mushrooms as countless anglers of several nationalities vied with each other to catch monster carp. Now in our Midlands there are a number of trout reservoirs, most have pike in them and most have produced big pike. Unfortunately, due to netting, cormorants and sometimes plain bad luck many of these trout waters are not particularly good as big pike waters, but, fortunately, there are a couple that have come up trumps. The most famous of all must be Blithfield Reservoir, near Rugeley in Staffordshire. This water has single-handedly rewritten the pike record books; it still has not produced the biggest pike to be caught in the United Kingdom, but there have been more thirty-five-pounders from there than from any other water.

Before I describe how to tackle the water, a little history: in the mid 1980s I worked for the National River Authority, eventually to become the Environment Agency. As part of the fisheries

The notice board at Blithfield.

team, it had been my job to assist in the netting of the reservoir for coarse fish. Although it was hard work we sometimes got the net around some amazing hauls of roach. I remember one netful of 1lb-plus fish, which was too much for us to deal with as we had only one fish transporter. We had to come back the next day to make a second trip. We turned a few pike up as well, but nothing huge. Because we had helped Blithfield Anglers by netting the reservoir and, presumably, paying them something for our catches, when the reservoir opened for pike fishing the pike enthusiasts on the team were invited to fish on the first open weekend. The whole thing was a disaster. The pike-fishing experts (us!) caught very little, while the trout anglers casting Big S and Toby lures from the bank had a field day. The result was a lot of dead pike to 21lb.

Subsequently, we got our acts together and eventually caught some good pike. My best two went to 31lb and 29lb 15oz. Then, because people were turning up uninvited, killing trout, using livebaits (it was lures and deadbaits only) and putting pike back (they were supposed to be moved elsewhere), the fishing was stopped.

Until the late 1990s, the pike fishing at Blithfield remained a closed shop and very exclusive with only odd bits of information coming out about what was being caught. We did hear about the odd exceptional fish such as Paul Harvey's 42lb 10oz, fly-caught pike and some of the other big ones he caught during the trout anglers' odd days' pike fishing.

Then, out of the blue, Nige Williams finally managed to strike a deal with Blithfield Anglers to form a sub-section of the trout club intended specifically for fishing for the pike. It was not going to be cheap at £300 for eight days' fishing, but for many of those who joined the club as pike members it was going to change their pike fishing forever.

Many readers of this book will have had his or her appetite whetted by the stories of the huge pike that have been caught from Blithfield. How then do you get to fish there and how do you fish it? Two people control the waiting list for membership there. One is Nige Williams himself, the other is John Davey. John's association with Blithfield is through the Staffordshire Predator Group, a collection of pike-minded anglers from the Stoke-on-Trent area. He is also the bailiff at Rudyard Lake in Staffordshire; to get on the waiting list contact either of them. But remember that it is not cheap – the price in 2004 was £360 for eight days but it also includes the use of a boat and engine. The waiting list can vary in length and probably depends on how the fishery has performed in the previous season. My view is that if you want a challenge and the chance of a very big pike then Blithfield has to be worth serious consideration.

What then of the fishing? Well, in the past five years this trout water has produced a huge number of 35lb-plus pike, including the British record brace of 41lb 8oz and 37lb 8oz to Eric Edwards in October 2001. It is not easy and a lot of members have struggled. During the five years, I have had just one over 20lb, an odd-looking, twenty-seven-pounder that appeared to have been stuck in a fence at some time in its life. Not much of a return for about £1,600. Luckily, I caught my 31lb and 29lb 15oz in the earlier years.

I shall now take the reader for a tour around the reservoir. It is around 800 acres in size and situated near to the village of Abbotts Bromley. If you drive down to the fishing lodge, which is situated at the south-west corner of the reservoir, you are where the boats are kept. The reservoir is divided into two by a causeway, which carries the Abbotts Bromley to Rugeley road. Generally, the reservoir when at full level is seldom deeper than 40ft, much of it is less than 25ft deep. It is therefore ideal for trolling lures or, if the pike are even shallower, casting lures.

Looking up the reservoir on the west bank from the lodge, the first notable feature you come to is where a fence comes down to the water. What makes this area attractive to pike is unclear, but it did not stop Jason Davies catching a thirty-five pounder off the bank there in February 2002. Further along the bank is a bay called Ten Acre Bay. It is fairly shallow and, when water levels are high, it is 6 to 15ft deep. Quite a few big pike have come out of it including Nige William's thirty-two pounder while I was acting as ghillie for him. It is best fished by casting although you can troll in and out of it if you watch the echo sounder closely. Just as you head out of the bay, turning left, there is a sunken island with a nasty snag on it. It looks a good area and I am sure it is, but all that has ever happened to me is that my lures have got snagged.

John Davey with a Blithfield 'biggie' at 37lb 8oz. It succumbed to a trolled lure, a Joe Bucher Shallow Jointed Raider.

Heading up the reservoir the bank looks fairly featureless, but there is one spot by a fishing shelter that has produced the odd big fish from the bank and to boat anglers casting towards it. Further along is St Stephens Bay, which has been the scene of many big-pike captures, including Paul Harvey's huge fly-caught 40. Most of the big pike caught in St Stephens have come to trollers who invariably pass through on the way around the reservoir. Before long you then arrive at the first corner by the causeway. This has produced good pike, but I have never seen nor caught one there myself. The causeway itself has produced lots of big pike to trollers, including a thirty-five pounder to Jason Latham who was ahead of us at the time. As you progress along the causeway you pass through the channel that connects the two sections of the reservoir. Here it is around 25ft deep and often there

are large shoals of prey fish in residence. Big pike have been caught here, but, needless to say, not by me! Passing by the gap, you end up working along the causeway again. Generally, the first few hundred yards tend to be pretty poor, but eventually you will come to perhaps the most famous corner in pike-fishing history.

They call it Watery Lane and it has certainly brought water to the eyes of lots of people. For about 200yd from the corner back towards the dam of the reservoir is a stretch of water that has produced some incredible fish. Mick Brown's personal best thirty-five pounder was caught there, along with Mark Ackerley's 37lb 4oz. James Gardner had a 35 here and Ernie Latham trolled past and took a 36lb 2oz. My contribution here was the 29lb 15oz during the early days, but Nige Williams had a 35lb-plus fish follow his Castiac lure, which was tangled at the

Some of the Blithfield line-up, bank fishing at Watery Lane.

time, right up to the surface. My Magnum Dawg was grabbed at the side of the boat by a 30lb-plus fish. All it left to remind me of it was a set of teeth marks in the tail. Many other twenty and thirty pounders have been caught in this small area, yet no one really understands why the pike like it so much. Perhaps the prevailing south-westerly winds attract the trout and then the big pike. It is certainly true that there are always plenty of trout showing in this area.

Heading further back towards the dam you come to a large bay we call 'the concrete bowl', because the sides of it are lined by ... you guessed, concrete. This area has produced a thirty-four and a thirty-two pounder in recent years, but has always let Nige and me down big time. The rest of the bank down to the sailing club bay tends to be rather shallow and does not have much of a track record. The sailing club bay has produced a few doubles and the dam itself has produced the odd surprise thirty pounder, but generally the sailing club bay and the dam have been hard work.

Moving on to the upper part of the reservoir, there are two arms. During 2002 and 2003 the Staffordshire Water Company were using nets of barley straw strung across the lower part of the reservoir to attempt to control algal blooms. This has somewhat restricted the fishing in part of the reservoir, although it has not really affected the results overall. On the west bank, heading up the arm, is a fairly featureless stretch of bank, which interestingly has produced some very big fish, usually to anglers keen to get away from the more popular stretches on the east banks. The north-western arm of the reservoir rapidly becomes very shallow and, when water levels are high, some good fish can be found in the sunken trees. I have tried it umpteen times but only had a handful of jacks.

The other arm is where many of the big pike have been caught. As already mentioned, shores which receive the prevailing wind frequently seem to be better for pike than the ones in the lee. The north-eastern arm is separated from the other one by Beech Tree Point, again, not the best big pike area, but all spots on Blithfield have

their day, as Jason Davies found when he caught a thirty-seven pounder there. Round from Beech Tree the reservoir is a nature reserve, so a quick dash over the other side takes you to the Duckleys, and here begin about 700yd of brilliant pike fishing. The Duckleys itself probably fishes best when water levels are high. Casting lures such as Squirreley Burts right into the overhanging trees has turned up some very big fish to over 36lb. On another day, when the water levels have been low, results have been very poor. Part of the secret of coming to terms with Blithfield is sorting out the influences of the time of year, the water levels and the water temperatures. Sadly, I seem to be a bit behind the times in doing this, but I am still trying hard.

Down from the Duckleys there is a section of bank that has been protected by stone-filled gabions. Known as Yeatsall, this is where Eric Edwards had his biggest brace of pike. It has produced both from the boat, casting towards the bank when water levels have been high or low, and also when bank fishing has been allowed. Big fish have turned up consistently there, my thirty-one pounder from the early Blithfield era came from here. The lines of barley straw bales can be a nuisance, but it is possible to anchor up between them and, provided that you can cast straight, fish each lane effectively. You can also troll up and down them. Finally, we reach the corner by the causeway and this is nowhere near as consistent as the corner at Watery Lane. However, you can never rule anywhere out on this fickle water.

Other than casting, lots of anglers choose to troll a variety of lures such as Bulldawgs, Super Shads, Storm Deep Thunders and Depthraiders. Pike can be picked up in 10 or 20ft or at any depth in between. I watch what other anglers do when trolling, but, unfortunately, I have yet to catch a Blithfield pike of any size on the troll. I know most of the theory, but do not seem able to put things into practice. Knowing when to troll and when to cast are things I am trying to come to terms with. At present, early in the fishing season in October and November it seems to be mainly casting, while February–March is trolling time. The pike obviously change their habits as the water temperature falls and, in order to catch them, we have to follow their behaviour patterns and react accordingly.

Blithfield is probably the greatest leveller in pike fishing. A few people with inflated egos have come up against the curse of Blithfield. Others are perfectly competent pike anglers, but luck seems to pass them by. But one thing is certain: the number of waters with the potential to produce pike in the 35 to 40lb range is very limited. For that reason alone I shall continue to fish there.

Ladybower Reservoir

The other significant trout water in the Midlands is Ladybower Reservoir. Situated up in the Pennines to the west of Sheffield, Ladybower is one of the few put and take trout fisheries which have been established on an upland reservoir. The trout fishing has existed since the end of the war, but the pike appeared only in the 1980s. How they got there is anyone's guess, but the hand of a local pike angler cannot be discounted.

My involvement with the pike fishing there is well documented elsewhere and so, rather than give the reader a history lesson, I shall describe the reservoir and then give an idea of how to go about fishing the water. The biggest single thing most pike anglers struggle with on Ladybower is the depth. The fact that most of it is over 40ft deep down to 130ft throws many anglers. The simple answer to this problem is that you ignore the deep water. The water level also has a bearing on where you fish. Although water levels can easily vary by 40ft, let me first describe the good areas when water levels are at their maximum. Locating the pike is rather simple, they will be in less than 10ft of water. Because there are few food fish other than rainbow trout in the reservoir, the pike usually live in areas that allow them to have the best opportunity of catching one of these bars of silver with the minimum of effort. Rainbow trout tend to spend a lot of time in the surface layers. Pike, on the other hand, frequently sit on the

bottom waiting to lunge upwards at a trout. The shallower the water, within reason, the easier it is for a pike to catch its prey.

If you go up the arm of the reservoir which follows the A57 you come to where the Snake River comes in. The river carves a deep channel for about 600yd. On either side of this deep channel (down to 25ft) are areas of from 5 to 7ft of water. These consist of mixtures of sand and mud, and these areas are the ones to look for. On the A57 side of the end of the Snake Arm are lots of overhanging trees. Wherever the water is from 5 to 7ft deep, the pike here tend to use the overhanging trees for cover. They like a nice, flat bottom rather than rocks, which suggests to me that they do actually lie right on the deck. During the three years that I fished the reservoir a number of good spots became evident around the inflow of Snake River. Not all produced each time we fished there, but experience gradually taught us where the key areas were. Interestingly, we thought the gusher where water came in from Edale was the spot, especially after I had a 37lb 8oz from beside it. Unfortunately, Ladybower tends to play tricks on you and, apart from a twelve-pounder, that was the only double-figure fish we ever had from there.

Tactics at the end of the Snake Arm have had to change since we fished it. During our time there all you needed to do was lure fish. Most of the fish I caught fell to the humble Springdawg and Kussammo spoons. Some of the bigger fish fell to float-fished, float-trolled and float-paternostered livebaits, but once the reservoir was opened to the general pike-angling public, livebaits became the most effective method. Many people chose to float-troll livebaits, and, when you go back and forwards plenty of times, you may eventually induce a take from a pike. Sometimes the float-trolled livebait just does not work simply because the pike needs a bit longer to make up its mind. Then fishing static with free-swimming livebaits or float-paternostered baits is the answer. A pike has longer to make up its mind this way.

Away from the end of the Snake Arm there is a huge arm of the reservoir which can, from time

ABOVE: Ladybower when low water levels revealed its depths and features.

to time, produce the odd good fish. I have trolled up and down it with lures and livebaits and most of the time have caught absolutely nothing. Just once in a while, though, you will pick up a fish away from the end of the Snake Arm. One year I had two 20s on Bulldawgs, working from about 500yd from the Snake River back to the main A57 bridge. Needless to say, I never managed to repeat this feat.

When water levels are high my experience has been that the main basin of the reservoir is a complete waste of time. But someone might prove me wrong one day, such is my lack of confidence in my own experiences; however, for the sake of this chapter I shall stick to these. The other arm of the reservoir, the Derwent Arm, is the most difficult one to tackle. There is little shallow water and, as you proceed up the arm

A fine Ladybower pike for Neville Fickling.

towards where there is shallow water at Fairholmes, you find your way blocked by a pipe viaduct, but despite this there is hope. About a mile up the arm on the east bank a small stream comes in. I have tried this repeatedly and in five years I have managed one jack run there, so I would not pin too much hope on this spot. About another half mile along a larger stream runs into the reservoir, this is Mill Brook. In our first year of fishing the reservoir this spot proved to be completely useless. That was until February, then the odd pike started to show there. Nige picked up a twenty-one pounder while I was fishing with him and a year and a half later, while fishing on my own in November, my first few casts yielded a twenty-two pounder. A few more casts with the same Springdawg saw a big fish follow me in right to the bank. It cleared off when it saw me, but a livebait cast into the area soon produced a run from what looked like a 30 as it powered around the shallows. It was not quite that big, but twenty-seven pounders are not to be sneezed at. Other than that, one low twenty and a fifteen pounder are all that Mill Brook has had to offer me.

As I said earlier, a pipe viaduct separates Fairholmes from the rest of the reservoir, which is bad news if you are a boat angler because you cannot usually get in there. However, water levels do tend to go up and down, and, provided that the reservoir is more than 3ft down, you can get a boat into Fairholmes. The key spot is where the small stream comes into the lagoon. Nige Williams had three of his 30s from the reservoir from this spot; my own best was 24lb. The area in front of the large car park can also produce, mainly because it is an area with a nice, flat, sandy bottom. My best here was 29lb. Further round the back at Fairholmes the inflow from the next reservoir, the Derwent, comes in. You can sometimes pick pike up around here but it is inconsistent. We had one seventeen-pounder there in the first two years and then in the third year a load of fish to 25lb. Once the reservoir was opened to regular fishing all the whole of Fairholmes has done is a twenty-five- and a twenty-one-pounder. It is a very strange water.

When the water is 40ft down all the hot areas at the Snake River, Mill Brook and Fairholmes are dry land. The pike then take up residence in totally different areas. Because I had never fished the reservoir when it was 40ft down, the first year it was opened to general angling I was as lost as the next person. Little wonder then that I struggled to catch at the previous rate when the reservoir opened. What threw me was the fact that the big pike took up residence over the same features as they did when the reservoir was high. Once again, flat, smooth, sandy bottoms in less than 10ft of water were what the pike wanted. The fact that these areas were nearly at the landing-stage end of the reservoir confused me completely. By the time I had realized what was going on I had missed out on the best of the fishing. I did pick up a couple of 20s at that end of the reservoir, but it should have been more. As the water level came up gradually the pike left this area and started to come out in their high-water-level areas.

One thing that has concerned me about the fishing there is the fact that we had few repeats. None of the eight thirty pounders it produced were caught again. Very few of the 20s reappeared either. This appears to be perfectly normal on many trout waters. We did have the odd recapture, including a twenty-seven-pounder I had twice. Where they go to concerns me. Do they really go somewhere else and avoid getting caught again, or do they die and sink to the bottom never to be seen again? Until someone attaches some radio tags to pike that have been caught on rod and line there we shall probably never know. My feeling is that these fish are very fat and the water chemistry is such (possible low pH) that they may be enormously stressed simply by being caught. I can find no evidence to support this hypothesis, but the circumstantial evidence suggests that an awful lot of big pike turn up only once. On a water where the pike probably grow at a phenomenal rate this is not likely to be a problem, they simply replace their lost brethren. Again, there is no proof of my theory, but I think that once pike have got to a stock-trout eating size of, say, 8lb, at probably three or four years old, they may be able to grow at perhaps twice the rate we once thought was tops for trout waters; let us for argument's sake say 8lb a year. What the true ceiling could be is anyone's guess. Another two years at 8lb a year and we are closing in on the present Llandegfedd record. Unfortunately, you have to be a very lucky Ladybower pike to avoid problems at spawning time and perhaps also getting caught. It may be hoped that the next few years will provide more information.

Incidentally, there is a precedent for a pike growing at 8lb a year because Mark Ackerley had a 12lb Mask pike that he caught again at 20lb in the following year. Unfortunately, that fish came out again at 20lb in the next year. However, if a pike can grow 8lb in one year it ought to be possible to see the same leap happen in two or even three years on the trot. Be that as it may, because I now turn to a more natural fishery.

The River Trent

The Trent is one of the biggest waters in the country and I cannot pretend to have mastered it in any way at all, I have merely scratched the surface and in so doing caught a few fish up to a desirable size along the way.

The river has changed a lot since I first came to live in Gainsborough. When I arrived we were just coming to the end of Britain's association

The Trent, meandering its way through Nottinghamshire and Lincolnshire.

with the smokestack industries that had turned many of our rivers into piscine wastelands. The mammoth clean-up of our waterways had only just begun and any river that flowed through large industrial areas was at best grossly polluted and at worst totally devoid of life. Nowadays, following a massive effort at water-quality improvement it is a vastly improved fishery. In the 1980s the river was artificially warmed by the many power stations that used its water to cool the steam from the turbines after it had finished generating electricity. Though the water was no longer badly polluted by industrial chemicals, the load of treated sewage effluent was still considerable. Rather than damage the fishing this artificial enrichment served to provide food for a far greater head of fish than would ever be naturally supported. Gudgeon and roach abounded, along with lots of chub and silver bream. Pike did not thrive perhaps as well as they could because I am pretty certain that they like clean water. A big input of sewage effluent tends to see periods of low oxygen level, something of which pike are much less tolerant than, say, gudgeon and roach.

Moving on, before dealing with the main areas of the Trent that I have pike-fished, it must be pointed out that there are other good stretches for pike further upstream. For example, Beeston Weir, near Clifton, south of Nottingham, has good pike in the weir pool itself, as has the deep, slow-moving section of the river at the embankment upstream of the City of Nottingham (and it is free fishing here). Indeed, even the slower sections of the upper Trent have a head of pike. But having said this, I want to concentrate on the section of the river that I have been most involved in, namely the tidal river below Collingham (or Cromwell, as it is also known) Weir Pool; essentially it is the area between Newark and Gainsborough.

When I started to fish the tidal Trent for pike in the late 1980s, I, like many others, had heard the constant tales of big pike but never with any evidence. The hotspot on the tidal river appeared to be the last weir pool before it entered the Humber, namely Collingham. It took a long time

before I finally got around to trying to fish there, but I did know one section of the river about 3 miles downstream from Collingham where I could drive to the bank and then launch my 9ft boat. On the day in question, after a dawn start, it took an hour and a half to reach the weir pool. I almost died of boredom. Still, the effort was worthwhile as I had seven pike over 10lb topped by a seventeen-pounder. The fish fell to either sunken float-paternostered livebaits or wobbled deadbaits. Primed with that result, I proceeded to find somewhere closer to the weir pool to launch. Eventually, as luck would have it, I found a lonely hermit who lived right on the banks of the river and he allowed me to launch there. It was then only a matter of a 15min sprint up to the weir pool. But enough of this history, what did I discover about the tidal river?

Funnily enough, the more I explored the river the more confused I became. The first ever pike session was by the side of Dunham Bridge. Downstream of the bridge on the west bank there is a small slack, which looks as if it might attract some pike. That first session there, using livebaits, saw me catch several fish up to 9lb and naturally I was convinced that I had made a discovery that was going to keep me in pike for a number of years. That, alas, was not to be. I never had another good day there, although I suspect that it might actually fish better when the river is a couple of feet higher than normal.

Looking upstream from Dunham Bridge, about a mile upriver there is the most amazing, wide U-bend they call the Dubbs. My first trip there from the bank yielded a brace of low double-figure pike. The area has considerable variations in depth, being anything from 5 to 20ft deep and there is a huge slack where the current reverses. During September and October the whole area is full of roach and bream, and being there in a boat at dawn the sight of porpoising bream is a fascinating experience. I cannot tell the reader when the best time to fish this area is simply because I have still not yet determined it. However, others who are prepared to launch a boat by the bridge might be able to unravel the mysteries of catching the pike from this area.

With the number of food fish present there, there must surely be some good pike to be had.

Nearer to home and further downstream is another interesting area. At Torksey Lock the Fossdyke Navigation joins the Trent. Here, for about three-quarters of a mile an inlet of the Trent runs between the confluence with the river and the lock itself. This area is popular with the maggot anglers and attracts lots of small fish when the river is high. I have fished it quite often and had a few doubles to 16lb. It can produce fish to over 20lb, which a young lad named Ashley who used to help out in the shop found out. The river was up and his half mackerel was taken by a lovely, fat fish of just over 20lb. Other local anglers fishing in similar conditions have had fish to 23lb and, although not an inspiring spot, it can produce good fish. You can buy a day ticket to fish on each side of the inlet which we call Torksey Arm; they are sold on the bank. In the river itself the pike are difficult to locate, yet once in a while you can have a good day's sport. I was doing a spot of lure fishing one day where the arm meets the Trent, perhaps the most obvious spot, when I stumbled on a small pack of pike. I think I had six doubles up to 14lb on Bulldawgs and Springdawgs all in the one spot. Subsequent trips were not so productive and in the end I even tried trolling the whole area for several miles up and downstream but without much result.

Below Torksey, the influence of the tide starts to see the water more and more coloured and, although I am sure pike are present, it would be a brave angler who spent much time there. Over the years I have tried a lot of other areas, mainly fishing from the bank and surprises do happen from time to time. My friend Dave Moore was bored having little success barbel fishing this particular morning and so he dug out his pike rod and a small spinner, proceeding to try for some chub. I do not recall whether or not he had any, but he did manage a 23lb pike. That was on a stretch a couple of miles below the weir pool.

The weir pool itself is the easy place to catch a decent Trent pike. In the late 1980s I fished there regularly, usually only for mornings and usually only when everywhere else was frozen. Fishing paternostered livebaits, I had as many as five doubles in a short while, including a fish of 22lb 10oz. Times are different now. For one thing, we no longer get cold snaps and the river is a lot cleaner and not as warm as it was. These changes, coupled with the invasion of cormorants, have seen the food supply of the pike changed. Rather than roach and silver bream predominating, there are now more barbel and common bream. This means that the smaller pike initially have a more difficult time of it. But, once they get big enough to tackle the larger prey fish, then they can grow and I am sure the top weights we saw in the early 1990s of 25 to 26lb fish may well be exceeded. You did not get much action on the deadbaits, but now you can catch quite consistently on them, even in the weir pool.

I do not fish the weir pool now simply because it is a little too busy for my liking. While it can be fished from a one-man boat launched well downstream of the weir on the Cromwell bank, I would warn anyone of thinking of doing so that it is dangerous. You must wear a lifejacket and you must have a good quality anchor which will hold out in the middle of the river. You certainly do not stand up in an 8 to 10ft boat. You would be far better off buying a decent aluminium boat of, say, 14ft and fish with a mate.

My tactics would generally involve fishing around the pool using one rod with a paternostered livebait and another with a trotted livebait. If the trotted livebait fails then I simply add more lead and fish the same rod over-depth with a deadbait. I have done reasonably well with lamprey in the weir pool. Wobbled deadbaits also pick up fish, as do lures. Most of the regulars, though, swear by a good-sized livebait, but where you get them from these days is anyone's guess. Generally, the best spots are along the wall with the salmon pass, but sometimes you are better fishing as far down as the lock cutting itself. A few zander are starting to appear in the weir pool, although whether the Trent will give the Severn a run for its money remains to be seen.

An early Trent 20 for Neville Fickling. It weighed in at 21lb 10oz and was caught in freezing conditions.

There is a vast amount of scope on the Trent for someone to specialize in pike fishing. I keep meaning to try this, but I am constantly distracted by easier waters or by waters that have thrown up big fish. Exploration is not helped by the lack of a public slipway on the tidal river. If I could launch my big boat there it would be much easier to explore the river. Unfortunately, short of hiring a crane, that is not going to happen. But I really do hope that someone takes on board what I said here and gives it a proper try.

To conclude, there is a lot of scope for some good, even great pike fishing in the English Midlands. The possibilities range from small ponds and drains, through canals and lakes, to large reservoirs and a massive river. An account such as this can provide only an outline of the opportunities, but I hope that I have at least provided a taster, particularly with regard to some of the big-pike waters in this area of the country.

5 YORKSHIRE RIVER PIKE

Steve Rogowski

As the *Lonely Planet* guide to Britain states, the first thing to note about Yorkshire is its size. A second, though, is that the piking can be very good, despite some recent concerns about the River Ouse. Beginning with the first point, the county is so big that it is split up into the four separate entities of North Yorkshire, West Yorkshire, South Yorkshire and the East Riding. Yet it has a basic homogeneity and Yorkshire people have a confident 'national' pride that is lacking in many other parts of England. They, including myself, often refer to it as 'God's own country', this perhaps arising from the feelings of space and freedom that go hand-in-hand with sheer size. This sense of statehood is evidenced by Leeds United fans being almost as likely to chant 'Yorkshire, Yorkshire, Yorkshire' instead of referring to the city itself. In turn, this leads to the county's reputation for straight-talking, thrifty people, generations of whom struggled to make a living from the land or the factories. As such, Yorkshire prospered on the medieval wool trade, which helped to build York's great cathedral and immense monasteries such as Rievaulx and Fountains. Centuries later Leeds, Bradford and Sheffield became centres of the Industrial Revolution. Against this social story we have the Yorkshire countryside itself, which provides a great backdrop. There are the wild moors around Haworth, immortalized by the novels of the Brontë sisters, the delightful picturesque valleys of the Yorkshire Dales, the whaleback ridges and steep escarpments of the North York Moors, and the gently rolling countryside of the Yorkshire Wolds. And returning to the second point, all such areas have rivers that contain lively, rod-bending pike.

Steve Rogowski with a nice 17lb 12oz Yorkshire river pike, caught on a float-paternostered live chub cast into a deep pool with overhanging trees.

It is in the glacial valleys of the Pennines that shallow, fast-flowing brooks, or becks as we Yorkshire folk call them, provide the start of most Yorkshire rivers. They then flow eastwards towards the Vale of York, gradually deepening and slowing as they near and eventually join the Ouse. Further east, other rivers such as the Derwent and the Hull also start as brooks, in the North Yorkshire Moors and the Yorkshire Wolds, respectively, before slowing and meandering through the Wolds to the Ouse in the first case and the Humber estuary in the second. All these rivers are home to perfectly conditioned and streamlined pike. The hard-fighting nature of these fish surely makes up for the fact that it can be hard to catch a 20 and the very occasional 30lb pike.

This chapter outlines factors that have helped me come to terms with catching Yorkshire river pike, including descriptions of some memorable catches. I look at when and where to go, locating the pike, and rigs and tactics including baits. I then comment on recent suggestions that Yorkshire river piking, at least as far as the Ouse is concerned, has declined. Finally, despite the foregoing, I end on a positive note by describing a great day's piking there.

When to Go

In considering when actually to go pike fishing on these rivers, one has to bear in mind that they are affected more quickly by changes in conditions, and especially rain, than other waters. Thus they can become difficult to fish within a few hours, and the Ouse is prone to flooding in autumn and winter, so if you are travelling there from any distance it is best to check with the Environment Agency before setting off. There are other weather factors also to consider. For example, in my experience melted snow water entering rivers means that the pike fishing can be hard. Equally, bright, hot, sunny days can also be less than productive. On the other hand, rivers often tend to fish well after a sharp overnight frost or when they are fining down after a flood.

Of course, most of us cannot pick and choose when we go piking so we have to put up with whatever the weather decides to do. In reality, there are no hard and fast rules governing pike behaviour; they do have a habit of turning up in what might be considered adverse weather conditions. For example, I have had pike to over 20lb on hot, sunny days on the Ouse. Hence then my advice would be to note the less than ideal conditions referred to, but never be totally put off by them.

Mention should be made about the moon's phases and the effect these might have on pike fishing. There is a heated debate about this and there is no doubt that the moon affects tides and hence fish, including pike, in tidal areas of rivers. For example, at high tide the character of the river changes, with slacks becoming pacy runs and clear water colouring up. But whether it should be considered as a serious factor more generally in deciding when actually to go piking I remain unconvinced. No doubt, however, the debate will continue.

As for the best time of day to catch pike, looking at my records I find that there is no readily discernible pattern. However, as a general guide, as with most fishing, perhaps early morning or dusk tend to be the best times for producing. Again, this is not a hard and fast rule and pike can be caught throughout the day and even into the night. They often turn up very unexpectedly.

Mark Goddard and I once set our rods up on the Ouse at 5.0 a.m., but by mid afternoon neither of us had had any pike action. But around 3.15 p.m. he noticed a slight beep on his bite alarm and a run quickly ensued. This resulted in a struggle with a lean mid-double which eventually came to the net. Soon after he had another run quickly striking home and another hard fight ensued with this fine esox, splattering my face with white water as she came to the bank to be netted. It was another double, this time a sleek seventeen pounder. Feeling rather disheartened by all the action Mark was having, I quickly decided to change swims. I threw a couple of sprats near to an overhanging willow, and ledgered the same. Shortly afterwards, at about

Mark Goddard with a River Ouse mid-double.

BELOW: *Pike fishing against the odds – a flooded Yorkshire river swim. Even so, there is always a chance.*

3.30p.m., I had my only run of the day, which led to a nice, hard-fighting fifteen pounder which Mark quickly netted without being soaked. That was the end of the short, frenzied period, but it all goes to show that no matter how slow the day may seem there is always a chance of catching.

Where to Go

After we have decided when to go, it is obviously important to know where to go on the vast lengths of Yorkshire's rivers. It goes without saying that one can never guarantee that pike are going to be there, but the following provides a guide to piking areas on Yorkshire rivers. But it must be remembered that, as with most rivers, the upper reaches are home to trout and grayling, so it is on the lower stretches, where coarse fish including our quarry pike dominate, that I concentrate on.

Beginning with the River Swale, one has only to recall that Kenny Atkinson's thirty-five pounder was caught on here in 1996. It is below Richmond that coarse fish start to be found, initially dace, chub and barbel. Downstream of Catterick, especially as the river reaches Topcliffe, other species such as roach, bream and, not least, pike can also be had. Many regard Topcliffe as a Mecca for the coarse angler and this is not surprising. There are deep, quiet 'holes', long glides and eddies, which provide a perfect breeding ground for strong-fighting fish. Any of the deep-water stretches around here can produce pike and often do, while further downstream pike are to be had at Cundall and Helperby. Long twists and turns beneath sandy banks create eddies in which lurk some specimens. Indeed, this is an area where I recently found what looked like the ideal piking swim. It featured a large, deep, oxbow bend, with overhanging willows and bushes, a sunken tree and weedy glides. Sure enough, soon after casting in the baits a superbly marked, hard-fighting pike was landed.

Wensleydale is the home of the River Ure, with chub and barbel making their presence felt as the river slows around Wensley village. By Middleham the river becomes a good mixed fishery, with the trout and grayling being joined by coarse fish more generally. Further downstream, pike begin to show, not least at Ripon, which is one area in particular where I have had success. From here through Roecliffe, Boroughbridge and Aldborough to the junction with the Swale, coarse fish including pike come into their own. There are wide bends and sandy banks with deep slacks, often with overhanging willows, which provide ideal pike-holding areas.

It is downstream of Killinghall that the River Nidd broadens and slows in preparation for its meeting with the Ouse. Here coarse fish start to appear and at Knaresborough the water slows further, creating much deeper glides and pools where pike start to show in numbers. The weirs at Knaresborough itself are well worth a try. Further downstream the river becomes even more sluggish as it meanders through meadows. In these lower reaches, at places such as Little Ribston, Cowthorpe, and Moor and Nun Monkton, there are deep, silent eddies beneath sandy banks where pike fishing comes into its own. Little Ribston provided some success for one of my piking partners Karl Highton. He had devised yet another complicated paternoster-type rig which included the use of two wine bottle corks. I could not stop laughing as he baited it with a sprat and cast out, but the last laugh was on me as he soon landed what turned out to be the only pike of the day.

By Ilkley, chub appear on the River Wharfe and then, as the river gets to Wetherby, coarse fish become predominant, including pike. By Boston Spa the river becomes lazy, meandering between fairly high flood-banks. Such twists and turns gouge some wonderful deep eddies. Pike can be readily caught here as well as further downstream at Tadcaster and Ulleskelf where the river becomes tidal. It was at Tadcaster as a young teenager that I almost caught my first pike: I had actually caught a flounder and, as I was reeling it in, a jack followed close behind. At the time it got my heart thumping and I kept casting it out again in order to try and catch the snapper, but all to no avail.

This Aire 23lb 12oz fell to Peter Hague. A paternostered livebait led to this success.

The days of the Industrial Revolution are gone and now fish, including pike, are back in the River Aire and worth pursuing. By Skipton the river begins to become a good mixed fishery and after here it is the quieter eddies around Cononley, Kildwick and Steeton Bridge that produce pike regularly. But perhaps it is the river around Keighley where the chance of a specimen becomes more likely. By now the river often meanders through farmland and large pike can be had in the deeper water to be found at these oxbow bends. Indeed, this is where the Keighley Angling Club committee members Richard Young and Peter Hague have had pike to over the 20lb mark. Below here, Bingley and Shipley are the last stretches that are likely to be productive before the river continues on to the Ouse.

Brief mention must also be made of two other but lesser known rivers, the Calder and the Don. Although not renowned for pike, they are undoubtedly present. John Young reputedly caught a forty-pounder on the Don downstream from Doncaster, albeit that was in 1866! The Industrial Revolution then took its toll on fish stocks and hence pike on both of these rivers, but they have now recovered, so who knows what may happen in future?

All the rivers referred to eventually join the Ouse, which actually begins at Aldwark Bridge where the Ure joins the Swale and becomes the Ouse. It is a big river and can be very deep in places. Its proneness to flooding has been noted, and, apart from global warming being a factor, there is the huge volume of water from the Dales' rivers to consider. Nevertheless, it provides excellent sport for barbel, chub, perch, bream, roach, dace and coarse fish generally. It is not surprising that this is often regarded as the best pike river in Yorkshire. Linton Lock and Weir, for example, are full of fish including large pike. It can be busy in summer with boat traffic, so, despite the risks from flooding, autumn and winter provide the

A river personal best for Steve Rogowski, an Ouse 23lb specimen, which took a sunken float-paternostered live gudgeon.

best sport. And facing the River Nidd at Beningborough Park there is some of the best fishing on the river. This is a delightful water with deep and slow-moving stretches and overhanging trees and willows thereby providing some great pike-holding features. It is probably my favourite venue and it really can be excellent for pike fishing. Indeed, this is where I caught my personal best river pike.

I had arrived at the water on a cold, frosty but bright February day, with the river up a foot or so but steady. This was after quite a long, bracing walk around the gardens and grounds of a large, beautiful stately home owned by the National Trust. It had been quiet and peaceful with the only disturbance being caused when I had spooked a couple of wood pigeons that noisily fled the scene as I passed. I was now opposite the Nidd mouth where there is a lovely pool with a stretch of river-bank covered with sand. After scattering the mallards, I started by ledgering and float and sunken float paternostering sea and coarse deads, although it was not long before roach and gudgeon were being caught and used. I was really confident of catching even though the bite alarms remained silent for several hours. However, at 11.0 a.m. a single bleep and a shudder of the drop-back indicator made me think that an esox was interested in the sunken float paternostered live gudgeon. But it was more than interest as the alarm then roared away and I wound down and struck home into a large pike. As is often the case at this time of year, the fight was strong and determined rather than lively and spectacular, but I immediately wondered whether it could be a 20. After several minutes of rod-bent action, including fierce head and jaw shakes, a fine, plump specimen came to the net. 'Definitely a 20!', I thought, and, sure enough, it was, with the scales revealing she was 23lb exactly. Even though no further runs were forthcoming you can only imagine the celebrations I had in the local pub that night.

But it is not just at that pool that large pike are to be had. Further downstream, for instance, on the opposite bank the Redhouse–Killingbeck–Nether Poppleton stretch provides good sport as the river meanders and gouges deep runs often close to the bank. York city centre can also produce large pike, occasionally to over 30lb and especially in winter when the river is not in flood. In fact, large pike are liable to turn up anywhere along the Ouse, apart from perhaps the more obviously tidal stretches south of York.

Mention must be made of those two other good pike rivers in the east of the county, the Derwent and the Hull. The former sees coarse fish appear as the river arrives at Malton and by Howsham, through Stamford Bridge, Kexby, East Cottingham and Thorganby, the pike fishing really takes off. There are deep, slow oxbow bends along with weedy glides that readily produce. In addition, for example, I well recall trying a new stretch at Sutton on Derwent and finding a deep bend which really did cry out pike. Two ledgered mackerel head and tail baits were quickly cast and, though I had to wait a while, I was eventually rewarded with two fine, hard-fighting doubles within 5min.

On the River Hull it is Hempholme, Wilfholme, Aike and Arram, all upstream of Beverley, that provide good coarse fishing, including some large pike. It is not a large river and in summer the weed makes fishing difficult but it is still worth the effort. Again, the importance of its features needs to be emphasized, for example, where the numerous drains join the river. It was at Wilfholme that I recall losing a very large pike on a ledgered sprat cast to the mouth of a drain. As soon as I struck I knew that I was into a big fish and, although I had her on for a minute or two before the hooks gave way, I never actually

saw her. Downstream, towards Hull itself, however, the fish decrease in numbers as the river becomes more obviously tidal.

Locating the Pike

Not surprisingly, finding pike is the key to actually catching them. The foregoing has given some pointers in terms of where to pike on Yorkshire rivers, but, even when you reach such venues, how do you find the pike? I hope that the last section has provided some pointers, but here I attempt to answer this question more directly. Yorkshire rivers, like most rivers, tend to flow in a series of glides and rapids, which are interspersed by occasional pools of slow, deeper water. It is the latter that are likely to form holding areas, although in summer the pike are more widely spread. At this time of the year they move to areas of shallower water where their presence is betrayed by their crashing into shoals of prey fish, and casting baits to such areas can quickly bring success.

But it is the quiet, deeper pools that I have found to be the most productive, not least on the River Ure at Ripon, where my piking career began. For instance, a couple of miles or so downstream from the town itself the river becomes very slow, with depths running to over 12ft. There are lots of likely looking swims with features such as overhanging willows and other trees. I have had numerous enjoyable days here when many a pike has been had. Generally, they are not massive but they are hard-fighting and I have had many into double figures. On one occasion I recall watching my two rods, one of which had a sunken float paternostered live perch on and the other a ledgered dead roach. It was mid-morning on a lovely, sunny and warm June day. I had been there since dawn and had parked the car in my usual spot next to the farm. This had startled several rabbits and a hare but I quickly gathered my gear, climbed over a fence and headed over a dew-laden and lush green field to the river. I disturbed the sheep but they largely ignored me. On arriving at the water I had been greeted by the sight of mist slowly clearing and a pheasant being startled, and startling me. I had quickly tackled up and cast in two rods with deads, later using the live perch positioned next to one of the willows. Nothing had happened in terms of runs all morning. The lives caught on a feeder rod kept the interest going but by now I was beginning to dose off. Suddenly I thought that I saw one rod tip slightly shudder. 'It must be the perch', I thought, but a few seconds later there was a single bleep from the bite alarm and the drop-back twitched before what seemed like all hell was let loose. The alarm began screeching away and the drop-back clattered the bank-stick as I quickly got to

A sunken float-paternostered live roach led to this Ouse 22lb beauty for Steve Rogowski.

my feet. Thoughts of 'It's got to be a decent pike' went through my head as I picked up the rod and wound down before striking home. Line sizzled off the reel as she set off downstream. It really was a hard-fighting summer pike and, after netting her as quickly as possible, the weighing revealed that she was 13lb exactly. This was less than I had expected given the strength of the scrap, but it still made my day, along with a 5lb snapper caught shortly afterwards on a ledgered dead dace. Not the most spectacular day's pike fishing in terms of numbers or size but still enjoyable nonetheless.

Meandering through miles of rich farmland the Ouse itself is a quintessential lowland river and, as I have said earlier, it provides my favourite swim. A special day one February a few years ago readily springs to mind. I had arrived after the long walk at the wide, deep river bend at the Nidd mouth soon after dawn. As usual, the mallards had quickly scuttled back into the water and swum away. It was cloudy, breezy but mild, with the river itself only a little above normal and fining down. These were ideal conditions and I quickly set up my usual three rods – ledger, float and sunken float paternoster – all initially with deadbaits. At 9.30 the bite alarm with the sunken float-paternostered dead roach went and I was quickly into and landed a fine pike of 11lb. By now I was catching and using roach and gudgeon livebaits and a jack soon followed. Then, at 11.40, the alarm on the sunken float-paternostered live roach bleeped away and I struck into what seemed a solid snag. Or was it a large pike? It turned out to be the latter as a large head eventually broke the surface with jaws agape. After strong runs and rod-bent action, a large 'mama' of 22lb was landed and photographed by a passing friendly young woman. She had never seen a pike before, never mind a fish as big as this. I was equally pleased even though the day was not yet over by any means.

At 2.50 the paternostered float bobbed again as the live gudgeon did its work. However, this time I thought something was different about its movement. Sure enough, immediately afterwards it bobbed repeatedly, rose in the water and then disappeared into the depths. I was soon into what felt like another large pike. She did not produce quite as exhilarating a fight as the first, but on landing a short, fat specimen, full of spawn revealed herself. She was 20lb 12oz and I could not believe my luck nor, more appropriately, I thought to myself, my skill. Two 20s in a day is certainly good piking by most people's standards and I thought I deserved the swig of whiskey as I sat back and reflected on what had occurred. Then, at 4.40, the sunken float-paternostered live roach went again, followed by a lively tussle resulting in a nine-pounder. This was to prove the last of the pike action although I continued to catch roach, gudgeon and some dace and small chub. As I slowly packed the gear away, the mallards returned, now more friendly as they searched for discarded maggots and any other scraps of food they could get hold of. A couple of inquisitive swans did the same while I again contemplated an excellent day's pike fishing.

By now the reader will have realized the importance of features when it comes to catching river pike: weir pools and locks, quiet slacks, where side streams and rivers enter, overhanging trees and bushes, and deep oxbow bends. These are all potential pike-holding areas. For instance, weir pools are good pike-holding spots because oxygen levels are high there and prey fish congregate as a result. On the other hand, lock gates and similar man-made structures such as bridges produce because they provide cover as well as slack water. It must also be emphasized that they do not have to be large features. I recall my nephew Adam catching his first double on the Aire. He cast a ledgered mackerel tail towards a bush on the opposite bank. It did not take long for the optonic bite alarm to bleep hesitantly before he wound down, struck and landed a fine double-figure fish. Or again, I once arrived at a largish oxbow bend, also on the Aire, and immediately thought that the deep, slack water in front of me would be the area to produce. However, several hours later the baits remained untouched. I had earlier noticed a tiny beck which entered the river opposite to me on the far bank. At first I thought little of it, but as things

were slow I decided to cast a ledgered dead gudgeon towards the beck mouth. Sure enough, two pike were quickly caught, both on the same ledgered gudgeon. Admittedly they were only jacks, but they certainly helped to break up that day's piking.

Adam Rogowski with his first river double from the Aire; it was tempted by a ledgered mackerel tail cast towards a bush on the opposite bank.

Like many others, I have usually had success within a few yards of the riverbank rather than in the middle or on the far bank. This was certainly the case in most of catches described above. But, as the last paragraph indicates, this does not mean that the other areas of rivers should be neglected. Pike can certainly be found further out and near the opposite bank, taking advantage of the cover provided by such as small islands, weed and bushes. In short, any feature that breaks up the uniform nature of the river is well worth a try.

Rigs and Tactics

As far as rigs are concerned my motto is 'keep it simple'. This advice is meant for those who are always trying to dream up rigs. These, often complicated, all singing, all dancing rigs are often devised by armchair pikers (apologies to Karl Highton). I simply do not think that they are necessary. There are four basic rigs that I use: float and sunken float paternoster, basic running ledger and free roving/trotted float. Lure fishing and wobbling are only occasionally attempted, although to be honest I have had only limited success.

One of the best tips for embarking on a new river is to be prepared for being mobile. This means taking only the minimum tackle necessary to enable you to tackle up and cast a couple of rods. If no runs are forthcoming within an hour or so, you can then leapfrog the rods along the bank until the pike are found. Such mobility can also help to explain when and where to use the several types of rigs referred to above. For example, a first swim might consist of a deep glide, suggesting that a free roving or trotted float bait is the answer. Then again, you may come across a huge, fallen tree, which is half in the river. This is likely to hold pike but be difficult to fish, and so a float or sunken float-paternostered bait could do the trick since such rigs are useful in such tight, snaggy swims. Finally, you may come across a barge or a similar feature, so a ledgered live or deadbait cast along the side might lead to success. I once arrived at dawn to another of my favourite swims on the Ouse only to find that a large barge had moored there overnight. I worried a little about waking the occupants but did not let this put me off as I quickly cast a ledgered dead roach alongside the vessel. After an hour or so a single bleep from the alarm and a shuddering drop-back indicator led to a hard, solid scrap with a large pike. Several long, sizzling runs later she was finally netted with the weighing revealing a fine 21lb 4oz specimen, at that time a river personal best.

Varying the rigs (and baits) you use is another useful tip. After ledgering a dead sea bait on the bottom of a likely looking swim for half an hour or so, it may well pay to switch to trying a free-roving float with a live roach. Alternatively, after trying a float-paternostered deadbait next to an overhanging willow, you will be surprised how switching to a roach or perch livebait can often bring success.

When it comes to bait, as some of the above indicates, I usually start by using deads, either coarse or sea, until livebaits have been caught. All these work well, but the accepted view seems to be that lives produce more runs than deads, although they often tend to be jacks. Even so, it must be pointed out that I have caught lots of mid and high doubles on lives, and most of my river 20s were caught on lives. Not surprisingly, all live coarse fish produce and I have caught on most of them, although if I have any favourites it has to be gudgeon as they are certainly tough and lively little scrappers. The use of jacks also deserves a mention since frequently they seem to lead to a bigger pike soon after they have been cast out. As for deads, I have used most coarse fish with success, not least again gudgeon. All sea deads seem to work, with my favourite being mackerel, smelt and the humble sprat. It must also be emphasized that not all deads, coarse or sea, have to be ledgered, being equally effective suspended by free roving/trotted float or float and sunken float paternoster. Additionally, of course, it must be remembered that deads can be popped up off the bottom, for example, if there is a lot of weed which could otherwise hide the bait.

The Ouse in Decline?

The significance of the River Ouse in relation to pike fishing on Yorkshire rivers will by now have become apparent. It is the river most likely to produce 20 and 30lb pike, as well as numerous doubles and jacks. It is also the river where I have had most success. But over recent years there has been a suggestion that the piking is in decline. I first noticed this in conversations with fellow pikers along with what I thought was a decline in my catches. In particular, Dave

Greenwood, who has caught many pike, including a 30 on the Ouse, was concerned about the apparent decline. I decided to look at my records, analyse my success rate and raise the findings with the Pike Anglers Club. This was during spring 2003, when all I could recall catching over the previous year was a dwindling number of jacks and one mid-double. My records revealed a decline in the numbers and size of pike caught, although perhaps not as much as I originally thought. Furthermore, this decline related to the previous two years only. For instance, during the late 1990s I was averaging at times 2.5 pike per visit (and on occasions I managed up to twelve on a visit) and the ratio of doubles to singles was at times 1:3. Over the previous two years, I averaged only 1.6 pike

'Secretive' Dave Greenwood with a lure-caught 32lb 8oz from the Ouse.

per visit, and the ratio of doubles to singles was 1:24! All this could be seen as merely a blip in a single piker's career, but anecdotal evidence and talking to other pikers such as Dave Greenwood, suggested otherwise. And if the Ouse is in decline, why is it happening?

One answer I suggested was the more frequent flooding of the river during autumn and winter, which means there are fewer opportunities to go piking, or at least to go in optimal conditions. Other pikers thought that seals swimming up the Humber estuary and into the Ouse were to blame, and certainly during 2002 there was at least one seal present north of York to Linton Lock. In addition, I recalled, that following the summer drought of 1996, reservoirs in the north east were linked to West Yorkshire via the Ouse and many anglers warned that this could well affect the ecology of the river, including its future fish stocks.

Mark Ackerley thought that there may well have been a decline in piking on the Ouse, pointing out that the seal in Linton Lock had done untold damage to pike stocks by eating prey fish in that area. Similarly, Eric Edwards noted the decline in pike fishing, although he was more tentative about the reasons for it. Seal predation and wet winters he acknowledged could have had negative effects, but he gave greater emphasis to what he termed 'human predation'. More pikers on the river over recent times meant, he argued, more dead pike, baited hooks lost on snags, badly hooked pike and so on. Alternatively, he thought that the pike simply might not be in their old haunts as a result of the recent floods. These had torn up trees and moved big snags that used to hold pike, thus meaning that some 'banker' swims are now devoid of fish.

Chris Bielby, a biology student at Durham University, doubted that seals were causing a lot of damage to fish and hence pike stocks. However, he felt that the flooding might well have affected pike numbers since pike can be sensitive to water conditions. He also noted that changes in the Ouse's drainage basin were probably partly to blame for reduced numbers. The use of more agrochemicals, swifter drainage of urban areas and general changes in the drainage pattern of the river basin were all contributing factors, along with increased fishing pressure. Even so, Mark Ackerley was concerned that a grey seal eats about 5kg of fish, molluscs and crustacea a day. This means that, as Yorkshire river pike often spawn in weir pools, a seal resident there could have an effect on pike stocks over quite a wide area. Furthermore, a subsequent Environment Agency statement acknowledged that seals may occasionally damage fish stocks through predation, usually where there are barriers such as barrages or weirs against which to drive fish.

In a nutshell, then, it does seem that there has been a decline in the piking on the Ouse. Over the period June 2003–March 2004, although I averaged over 2.1 pike per visit, up on the previous couple of years, all were under 10lb. Some of the notes I made over the year are revealing. For example, a small jack was all a 10hr session in September produced, resulting in the comment that 'the lack of pike activity continues'. Five sessions in October and November resulted in nineteen pike but only to 8lb. This led to comments such as 'Glad to see the jacks are back so the biggies should arrive in February/March?' But sadly they never arrived, with only a few more jacks being caught.

There is likely to be a combination of factors related to this sad situation. For what it is worth, I now think that the impact of increased flooding, seal predation and Bielby's comments about changes in the Ouse's drainage basin are the most significant. And as I write, a report has recently been released about several fish species changing sex because of chemicals being released into rivers. Ultimately, this will have obvious repercussions in terms of fish stocks and therefore pike. Even so, I want to end this chapter on a positive note by suggesting that, despite the apparent decline, there are some grounds for optimism. First, during June 2004–March 2005 there was a slight improvement in that the average pike per visit went up to 2.5 and, in addition, the doubles started to reappear. This led to comments such as 'Nice to see the doubles are back so perhaps the mamas will also be back soon', though again, specimens never arrived. However, in November 2005 'Spinning' Steve Appleby had an eight-pike haul which included a fine 15lb 2oz falling to a rare, for him, fish bait as opposed to lure; float-ledgered herring tail did the trick. As a result, I maintain that the Ouse can still produce some good piking, as I hope the following shows.

The doubles are back on the Ouse. An eccentric 'Spinning' Steve Appleby with his 15lb 2oz that grabbed a float-ledgered herring tail.

An Ouse Piking High

Karl Highton and I arrived at the pool opposite the River Nidd at about 7.15 a.m. after the usual long walk. We decided, in an almost adolescent sort of way, to have a pike match. It was a mild March morning and the river looked perfect, being only about a foot above normal and slowly fining down. After the mallards left, we quickly set up the rods. I was in my usual swim next to an overhanging willow, while he was further down the beach-like area. He used a basic ledger rig and one of his own paternoster-type concoctions involving wine corks. I also ledgered and had a 'proper' float-paternoster set-up. As usual, we started with sea and coarse deads until the lives were caught. He was into the first action. Minutes after tackling up with his ledgered mackerel tail a run produced a pike of 6lb. Soon after, the bite alarm and drop-back on the same rod and bait went again, with his striking and exclaiming, 'It's a biggie!' The rod was bent solid so I gathered the net and, after a strong if not spectacular fight, she came to the net, with him proudly blurting, 'It's the biggest I have ever caught!' Indeed it was, with the scales revealing that this fine conditioned pike weighed 15lb exactly. He was really chuffed and, although it was still only early morning his hip flask of whiskey was quickly opened. It was going to be a great day we both thought as the dead roach on his other rod, the one with his home-made rig, was snaffled by a 7lb 8oz. We had been fishing for little over half an hour and he had managed three pike while I had yet to see any action. 'King of the Jacks' Highton was beating an experienced piker.

But I remained confident as gudgeon, roach and skimmer bream began to be caught and used. Sure enough, at 8.15 a 4lb jack succumbed to a float-paternostered live gudgeon. During the next couple of hours others, two of 6lb and one of 6lb 8oz, followed, also on float-paternostered lives. Interestingly, the two six pounders were the same fish, recognizable because of a small scar it had on its back. But Karl had three slightly larger pike up to 9lb, all on ledgered lives. We joked and laughed as the pike kept coming. even though by now he was a total of 30lb in front of me. It really was *Boys' Own* comic stuff! Over lunchtime two more pike of 5 and 6lb fell to me, again on lives with both rods catching, while he caught one of 3lb 8oz with his wine-cork contraption and a livey doing the trick. Though reduced, the gap was still over 20lb. By early afternoon things seemed to have dried up a little. I decided to change the float paternoster to a sunken one, using a live gudgeon in the process and pointing out that a change of rig or tactics often brings success. Karl doubted me, but at 3.00 the bite alarm on the sunken float paternoster screeched away. I was soon into a nice pike which on being netted weighed in at 12lb 8oz. The deficit was now only 10lb so it could still be anyone's match.

By 4.00 the discussion began to turn to when we were going to pack up. Karl was anxious to go as he was still in the lead and had seemingly won. Unsurprisingly, I was more hesitant. We compromised and agreed that we had had our last casts of the day, waiting in hopeful anticipation of a final run. Sure enough, within 10min my sunken paternostered alarm went again as a live bream had been taken. Almost simultaneously he had a run on a ledgered live gudgeon and quickly landed a 3lb jack. But I was into a bigger pike which fought much like my last one. On landing her we thought that it was the same fish although the weighing revealed that she was half a pound lighter. We decided to call it a day and quickly added up our totals: seven pike totalling 59lb for him and eight totalling 58lb for me. The friendly banter, packing up and return home began. That evening in the local pub Karl relished being the 'Pike King', no longer 'King of the Jacks', as he kept telling everyone about the day's events. Though not in the league of those who catch monster or hundreds of pounds of pike in a day, it still remains a memorable day's fishing.

In conclusion, I hope that this chapter at least provides a glimpse of some of the pleasures and attractions involved in fishing for Yorkshire river pike. But one must remember that, despite some of the comments in relation to the Ouse, Yorkshire rivers are often only relatively lightly fished for pike, with many anglers seemingly not realizing their potential. Admittedly a long walk to the river can be a chore, especially if one takes *all* that pike tackle, and clambering up and down muddy river banks can be a bit of a hassle when compared to some still-water pike fishing. Nevertheless, I will happily put up with such trials and tribulations as they are far outweighed by the thrills to be gained from catching these lean and toned fish. I shall certainly continue such piking with the aim, as always, being to catch that elusive, 30lb river specimen.

6 LAKE DISTRICT PIKE FISHING

Stephen Hincks

When I was asked if I would write a chapter on pike fishing in the Lake District I was more than happy to do so. I would class the lakes as my local waters, even though the south lakes are some 60 miles away from where I live, with the north lakes being over 100 miles away. The pike fishing around the Fylde coast is just so poor that the lakes are simply the nearest place for me to go for good quality pike fishing. You will understand if I do not write 'an X marks the spot' piece, rather this chapter provides a more general discussion of pike fishing in the area. Nevertheless, I do hope that the reader finds what follows of help in trying to catch hard-fighting, lakeland pike.

The Lake District National Park is an area of the country with outstanding natural beauty covering 880sq. miles. It attracts thousands of visitors every year. They are drawn by a magnificent range of mountains, together with deep glacial lakes such as Bassenthwaite, Ullswater, Coniston and Esthwaite to name a few. We must also not forget the largest natural lake in England, Windermere, which is 10½ miles long, 1 mile wide and has depths of around 200ft. All these mountains and lakes, as well as the varied fauna and flora, provide the area where William Wordsworth and Beatrix Potter resided, and where Donald Campbell lost his life on Coniston while he was trying to break the 300mph barrier in his powerboat *Bluebird*.

Apart from the large lakes, there are also small tarns, canals and rivers. Indeed, the Ulverston Canal, at 1 mile long, is the shortest canal in the country. The majority of these waters contain pike to some degree or another. Although there are some very large ones in the lakes, with quite a few 20s and odd 30s caught every year, 25lb-plus fish are still quite a rarity. A good percentage of

the 20s caught in the lakes are between 20 and 23lb, with the average size perhaps being in the 8 to 10lb bracket. But before we go into the tactics, tackle and the like, let me tell you about one of the first encounters I had with lakeland pike.

The Early Years

While still at school I was a member of a local fishing club, which rented a few ponds around Blackpool and the Fylde. Every year an out-of-town match was organized and in the year in question it was to be held at Bigland Tarn, a 13-acre lake near Haverthwaite in the south lakes. After the match started, it was not long before some of the members were experiencing problems as the resident pike took advantage of an easy meal by grabbing roach and perch as they were being reeled in. This increased my fascination with pike as I had always been interested in them even though I had not caught nor even seen one in the flesh. And then we had the weigh-in and, as the catches were being released, all hell seemed to break loose; the dazed roach and perch were being what can only be described as 'hammered' by the pike. The water surface repeatedly exploded as one after another roach and perch swam over the shallow ledge and straight into the jaws of old esox. This was the real beginning of my quest for pike.

As soon as I passed my driving test and got a car I knew that I would be back at Bigland. This I duly did and some great times were had catching plenty of fish up to low doubles. Sometimes I would even drive the 60 miles or so on summer evenings after work. These trips were the start of things to come, although it was not until 1990, a few years later, that I got more seriously into pike fishing. At the time, Esthwaite, a 280 acre trout lake near Hawkshead, was throwing some big pike up. I had fished it previously and caught lots of double-figure fish on lures but still had to catch my first 20. Before this I had joined the Pike Anglers Club of Great Britain and started to attend the local branch meetings at Blackpool, which was formed by two guys called Chris Ullyat and Graham Sleigh. The first meeting saw around half a dozen of us there and Graham seemed like a decent sort. We got on well and soon became fishing partners and good friends. A trip to Esthwaite was organized, which included myself, Graham and another member. We each took a small boat and set off float trolling with trout livebaits, which were sold on site. Things were uneventful until early afternoon when, in true lakeland style, the heavens opened

up. I headed towards the shore to find shelter under some overhanging trees and, as I neared the bank, one of the rods 'ripped off'. I thought that one of the rigs had caught on the drop-off but, when the boat hit the bank, the line was still pouring off my reel. It took me a few seconds to realize that it was a take. I hit it and pushed the boat back out into the lake. This fish was heavier than any other I had ever felt and I immediately knew it was a good pike. The fight lasted only a few minutes but seemed like an eternity with the fish in and out of the net twice. It was eventually successfully netted and turned out to be my first 20 at 21lb 4oz. After the fish was weighed I put it back in the net and lowered it into the water while two guys in a nearby boat came over to photograph it. An hour or so later I met with Graham and told him the good news. Congratulations eventually followed, although

Stephen Hincks with a typically fat Esthwaite fish.

initially he did not believe me, which was quite understandable since 20lb fish were a rarity for our group at that time.

Esthwaite proceeded to produce pike up to the upper 30s, including a fish of 33lb 4oz for Graham, which I netted for him. Unfortunately, I seemed to struggle and did not catch any more 20s, without doubt this being down to inexperience. For some reason I then left Esthwaite alone for a while to fish the Scottish lochs. We caught some good fish, but I wish that I had persevered with Esthwaite not least because, even though they do not seem to be there in the numbers they once were, 30lb fish are caught at least every other year. It must be remembered though that the pike are so well fed with the large stocking of trout and big shoals of coarse fish that it makes them difficult to catch and also that livebaits are no longer allowed, which makes things even more of a challenge.

Nevertheless, the point can be made that, if anything, it is now a little easier to catch on static deadbaits on Esthwaite. When it first opened for pike fishing the trout that were stocked were smaller than those of today since there were fewer cormorants around. These days the stocked trout are significantly larger, which makes them more difficult for the cormorants, and the pike, to eat. As a result, the pike are now quite happy to pick up deadbaits, at least until they grow large enough to be able to catch and eat the larger trout. But I digress a little as I now want to turn to how I now fish in lakeland.

Boat Fishing

I know that even the smallest of the lakes and tarns hold some good fish and are often overlooked, but my favourite way of tackling the Lake District is to fish the larger lakes by boat, using mainly lure-fishing tactics. But having said that, the deadbait gear is always with me in case an opportunity arises. A few years ago, when I got into lures in a big way, the deadbaiting gear was totally ignored. Even though my friends and I caught a lot of good fish I now

know that my not taking the bait rods was a big mistake; when you find a hotspot using the lures it often pays to get the deadbait rods out as well.

A key question is how do you get to grips with the larger lakes? Well, you either have to have some excellent information or put in the groundwork and fish your chosen lake week in and week out. I would go for the latter approach since I get a great deal of satisfaction in sussing things out for myself. To my mind, there is only one way to figure out a new lake and that is to troll, either with lures or float-trolling with baits. Trolling with lures will see you covering literally miles in a day, whereas float trolling is a lot slower and more methodical. Incidentally, the biggest mistake I see while people are trolling is catching a fish and then carrying on down the lake. Even if only a jack is caught my advice would be to give the area at least a once-over while having a good look at the fish-finder to see where the fish came from. Pike absolutely love features and will very rarely be swimming in the middle of nowhere.

Trolling lures or baits are a great way to cover lots of water on your first visit and to check out the topography at the same time. If you are trolling lures it is not a case of chucking a couple of lures out each and motoring off down the lake. You would be better advised to pick a depth band and stick to it. If you manage to cover the whole lake without catching try another depth band and go round again, and use similar lures in several colours. On some days the right colour choice can be the difference between success and failure. Speed can also be an important consideration. Recently one of my fishing partners and I kept such factors in mind on a new lake. We started catching fish after just a few minutes and found a fantastic hotspot after getting just a quarter way round the lake. But even if you catch nothing, pikey-looking areas can be marked for the next visit.

In many of the lakes there can be dozens of features, including drop-offs, a variety of weeds, weed edges, sunken boulders and reefs, islands, peninsulas, shallow and deep water. And you should not forget prey fish. But which areas do you actually fish? As a general rule, fish will usually be found on or near one or possibly two features on any given day. Knowing precisely which ones to fish will come only with hard work. As I suggested earlier, fishing a lake week in and week out and finding where the fish are early on in the session can bring great rewards with big bags of fish being taken. There have been times when the fish have been found early on and 200 to 300lb of fish have been caught on single-day sessions to lures. As an example, one particular recent session yielded forty-six fish over two days. This included twenty doubles to 19lb 8oz and four twenty pounders. But before you get excited and start hurtling up or down the M6, it must be noted that I have been fishing the lakes since 1990 and now have a good knowledge of the waters, swims, baits, lures, the times of the year and so on. But before this catch I was fishing this particular lake every week for at least two months, with little to show for the first month. Things gradually got better by the second month, until the pike went on a feeding spree, this lasting no more than a few days. I went back the week after and, even though I still caught, the sizes and the numbers of fish were considerably less than in the previous week, and in the immediately following week they had gone off completely. It is just like any water in the country – unless you are extremely lucky, you will only get out what you are prepared to put in.

If you are going to tackle the lakes by boat make sure that you have a sturdy vessel. You do not have to spend thousands of pounds, but you will need something that can handle the big waves and swells. You will also need a reliable motor, an optional electric motor, a good quality fishfinder, and ample ropes and anchors. There is nothing worse while being anchored up with a battery of rods out only to be blown off anchor. And do not forget to do your homework as regards engines; for example, on Windermere, Coniston and Derwent Water petrol motors may be used but a speed limit is enforced, whereas on Esthwaite and Bassenthwaite only rowing or electric motors are allowed. You should also bear in mind that, even in a strong wind, Esthwaite, especially the southern end of the lake, is still fishable with an electric motor, whereas to try this in a similar wind at Bassenthwaite would be dangerous. When the wind comes off the

This 25lb-plus fish took a liking to Stephen Hincks's trolled Depth Raider lure.

mountains at the latter it can be like being in a wind tunnel. On a number of occasions while fishing off the bank, for example, I have known the water have a slight ripple and then, in the next minute, the rods have been blown off the rod rests and shortly afterwards there will be white horses on the lake. So another key tip is that, if you are taking to the water at Bassenthwaite, for example, a reasonable forecast is needed.

My first boat was a 13ft, single-skin glassfibre model. It might have weighed a ton for its size but it was extremely stable and had lots of floor space. It lasted for a good ten years and was eventually sold and upgraded to a 14ft aluminium Sea Nymph with a semi-planing hull. These boats are incredibly stable and will cope with whatever lakeland weather can throw at them. They were designed primarily with lure fishing in mind but will also accommodate swivel seats, so when the deadbaits come into their own they are very comfortable, especially on cold, wet winter days.

At this stage I want to emphasize that lifejackets really should be worn at all times, even when the water is flat calm. I know that I am as guilty

as anyone for either forgetting to put mine on or taking it off in hot weather, but it surely goes without saying that to fall into freezing water can be deadly. In addition, I have seen yachts sunk, boats moored on the shore pushed through stone walls and wooden jetties smashed, so just imagine being on the water when the weather gets this bad. Please do not forget to wear your lifejacket!

With the rough terrain, dense weed beds and pike that will test any weak tackle, strong rods and lines are essential in the lakes. My boat rods for bait fishing are 10ft and 3.5lb test curve, coupled with Shimano 4500 baitrunners and loaded with 30lb Fireline. These are excellent at dealing, for example, with lunges from big fish heading for anchor ropes. For lure fishing I use two rods, one being a 6ft 6in jerkbait rod, an Abu Ambassador 6500 reel loaded with 100lb Power Pro braid. Some people think the latter is too heavy but it can be beneficial to the pike, especially in the warmer months when big fish can be landed, dealt with and back in the water in double-quick time, and if you cast a big jerkbait out and get a backlash, weaker lines will and have broken

A sturdy vessel is needed to boat fish the lakes.

whereas I do not have this problem. The other lure rod is a 7ft 6in, again with an Abu Ambassador reel but with 65lb Power Pro, this being a great rod for casting soft plastics and general lure fishing. Titanium traces that match the braid's breaking strain are used on both lure rods, this meaning that literally hundreds of fish can be caught on these leaders. When they become bent it is just a case of teasing them back into shape and changing the snap links once in a while.

As for the lures themselves, these days there are hundreds to choose from. They range from shallow and deep trolling lures, to lures for casting. The last include crankbaits, jerkbaits, pull baits, soft plastic lures such as Bulldawges and Castaics, spoons and spinnerbaits. I have a working collection of around a hundred but not all different, of course. Many are of the same

type but of a different colour and weight. It is really all down to your own preferences, these arising from gradually built up knowledge and experience. In the early years, while getting into lures, my mates and I have probably spent thousand of pounds on them, with at least half of them being virtually useless. Now we know what types to look for and very rarely buy a new type because what we already have will cover most eventualities.

The lakes are where I first got into lure fishing seriously. This was because after only a few weeks of lure fishing without the bait gear I broke my personnel best twice in a space of ten minutes. The first fish was 23lb 12oz, the second 33lb 1oz and both were taken on a 7½in, jointed Grandma lure in firetiger colour. After catching the 30 my mate Wayne Bailey said,

A lakeland 33lb 1oz personal best for Stephen Hincks.

'Now you have caught that you can lend me that lure.' I took it off and lent it to him with pleasure, but, unfortunately, we caught nothing else all day. After catching those fish it really was eat, sleep and drink lures, including reading anything and everything on them and lure fishing solidly for a couple of years.

If you are going to tackle the lakes with lures make sure that you have the right equipment for dealing with the fish. By this I mean good quality sets of long-nose pliers, hook cutters and a decent lure net. No matter what anyone may say, carp-style nets are just no good for netting fish with lures in their mouths. All it takes is for the fish to twist up in the net and you will have a huge task untangling things, which is not good for the fish at all. After catching lots of pike on lures over the years we now tend to hand land fish up to high doubles. Unless the fish looks like it might go over 20 the net stays put, and, unless you want a photograph, it is better for the fish if you guesstimate its weight and unhook it in the water. I must admit that I prefer to use a suede glove for unhooking (the 'paranoid glove', as it is known). This is because I was once unhooking a fish of around 8lb when it started thrashing and I got two barbed 4/0s in my hand, with the fish still attached and still thrashing. It was not a pretty sight.

Bank Fishing

The first point to note here is that for most of the time you will have to deal with rocks and boulders on the drop-offs. My rods then are 12ft and 3½lb test curve, with Shimano 4500 baitrunners, loaded this time with no less than 15lb Big Game mono. I tend to use just one rig and that is a float ledger or float paternoster. This is the same rig but with weak links of different length, a very short link on float ledger and an extended one on paternoster for getting the bait off the bottom. Using the float on the rig has two purposes: for keeping the line away from any potential hazards on the drop-offs, and for visual bite indication. Using a straight ledger is a definite 'no-no', unless you know for sure that the water in front of you is snag-free, which, in fact, is unusual. Weak ledger links here are essential. For instance, I remember bank fishing on Bassenthwaite not long after I started pike fishing, using 15lb main line and the same 15lb line on the ledger link. While playing a good pike, the link got stuck on the drop-off and would not break so that I could not land the fish. Luckily for the fish and me, Wayne was good enough to wade out and get a soaking to net it. This was the first and last time that this happened. Now I use cheap 8lb line for my ledger links, which seems just about right.

The rods are in on a typical lakes bank swim; note the rough terrain.

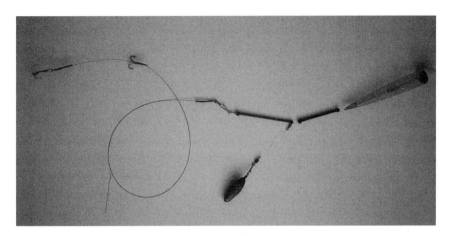

Stephen Hincks's float-ledgering rig.

While bank fishing I tend to use four rods where it is allowed. It may seem a lot but remember that you can be faced with a few miles of water as opposed to a few acres, so every extra assistance helps. Do not forget that, if you are going to use four rods, you must have sufficient licences. And as for gaining success from the bank, again persistence and groundwork will pay off. A good start is to get some Ordnance Survey maps. They can be invaluable, showing features such as peninsulas and bays along with tracks and roads, and not forgetting the parking areas. Concerning the last, at times it can be difficult to find somewhere to park, which sometimes leaves no option but to walk long distances to the swim.

The depths I tend to go for while bait fishing off the bank are usually between 20 and 30ft. By sticking to these you will not go far wrong in summer and winter. But having said that, lakeland pike have the tendency to turn up absolutely anywhere. I have had days in the depths of winter when three rods have been in the 20–30ft zone and a fourth rod cast into shallow water (under 10ft) and that is the one that caught the fish. At the other end of the scale, I know a couple of lads regularly taking fish in depths down to 80ft. It is just a case of being confident in whatever depth you are fishing. And just because it is summer does not mean that fish are always going to be in shallow water and because it is winter that they are always going to be in deep water. I tend to experiment throughout the day, go with my instinct and throw the rulebook out of the window.

Not Only Pike

Apart from pike there are other species of fish in the lakes that can be caught while pike fishing, namely brown trout, eels and perch. The brown trout (ferox) can be quite obliging, mostly in the winter, fairly regularly picking up deadbaits in deep water. I have had these to just short of double figures but know of authentic fish of 16lb plus. These are not as big as some of the big brownies that are caught in Scotland and Ireland every year, but I certainly would not say no to catching one. They can also be caught on trolled lures, mostly over deep water. It is important to note that great care must be taken with these brownies when unhooking and returning them to the water, they do not like being caught and die easily. If released too soon they will bolt off, only to float to the surface belly-up, so do not be too hasty to let them go.

Most of lakeland's waters are crawling with eels, with lots of small fish and a good number of specimens. Every year big eels are caught and, like the pike, seem to have a mad week or two, sometimes being a nuisance and taking lives, deads and even having a go at all types of lure. I have even caught them on jerkbaits. Before livebaiting was banned eels could be caught on 6in

It is not only pike; a near-double ferox trout for Stephen Hincks caught on a whole mackerel.

roach livebaits. One day Wayne and I had caught a dozen or so roach for baits and the first cast produced a 20lb 8oz pike. The fish was returned, another roach cast out and I instantly had another run which turned out to be a 4lb 4oz eel. Earlier that day Wayne had a 3lb 12oz eel, again on a livey. The perch are also present in large numbers in lakeland and are easily caught on small spinners with fish to around 1lb being common. These are mostly found in and around weed beds. Whenever fishing for perch please use a wire trace because, when you find the perch, there seem to be plenty of jack pike with them and they also provide good sport on light tackle. As well as the trout, eels and perch, there are massive numbers of roach in waters such as

Bassenthwaite, Rydal, Grasmere and Windermere as well as many smaller lakes and tarns. Every year these shoals become more prolific, with the average size increasing to around ¾ to 1lb, with fish of 2lb and more not uncommon. I am sure that anyone going after these and who sets his stall out properly could bag up big-time.

In referring to species other than pike, I must mention the Arctic char. These fish are a delicacy, being served in hotels and restaurants in the Lake District. While fishing the larger lakes the guys out in the boats fishing for char cannot be missed. They usually fish from loch-style boats and have big, long, bamboo canes with bells on the end, quite a sight if you have never seen this before. They fish with gold and silver spinners that can only be described as small mackerel spinners. These are set at regular intervals down to around 60ft. One char angler told me that the silver spinners he was using were made of the pure metal. Even though these are a deep water species, the average pike angler will be able to catch these elusive fish at certain times of the year when they move to the surface. For instance, lots of fish may often be seen topping over deep water and, although they are usually trout, occasionally they are char. When this occurs a small vibrax spinner with a ½ to ¾oz lead trolled fairly quickly will catch.

Friendships

Over the years fishing in the lakes I have fished with some great guys. As mentioned, for the first few years I fished with Graham Sleigh who taught me quite a lot about float trolling and generally helped me. Sadly, after a few years and a few disagreements we split the boat we shared and went our separate ways but still remain friends. After Graham I teamed up with Wayne Bailey, mentioned earlier, and we have fished the lakes together since around 1995 and caught a few good fish between us. Wayne's lakes' best stands at 31lb 4oz, although I was not there to see it. I had fished the venue the day before and, while fishing off some deep water, a fish I estimated as around a mid to high 20 followed a lure. I persevered for a few minutes but unfortunately it was not having any of it. Later during the evening someone I knew had a fish of 25lb from the same spot and I assumed that it was the fish that followed me. That was until the telephone rang at six the next morning. Yes, it was Wayne telling me he had just put a 30 back. Naturally, I was very well pleased for him, even if a little envious. Having been fishing together for around ten years we have hardly had a cross word and there have been some great times together. In fact, I have fished with quite a few people over the years but have often found that getting a good boat partner can be difficult. I have heard of people sulking because they are the ones not catching and others throwing the fish as well as their fishing equipment around for the same reason. I can quite honestly say that I am happy to be putting the net under a biggie for a mate and I am sure that the same goes the other way around.

More recently I have been fishing with Darren Lord, also a member of the original Blackpool Region of the PAC. His lakes' best is an Esthwaite fish of 29lb 14oz. It was caught not long after spawning and I think that a week on either side of catching it would have seen it go over 30lb. Even though he had just missed out on his first 30, I am sure that he was not disappointed with such a magnificent pike. Darren and I also fish with two top guys from down south, Tim Kelly and Martin Godlimen. Each year they come up to the lakes and fish for a couple of days with us. Martin has to be the clumsiest man I have ever met. Recently, while lure fishing on Windermere, he warned me of a big wash heading towards us from one of the ferries, but a few seconds later he had lost his balance because of the wash and ended up on his back on the bottom of my boat. Tim used to be a fly fisherman but changed over to lure fishing for pike a few years ago and has picked it up very quickly indeed.

More recently, my fifteen-year-old son Stevie has been accompanying us on our piking trips. He has fished for the last few years but has now been bitten by the piking bug. I have shown him the basics of handling, unhooking and the like and he now enjoys bank fishing. Wayne and I have been dropping him off at spots where we have caught from the boat. These are within easy reach of deep water but, with poor road access, they are usually under-fished. After a few sessions we had an excited call from him and returned from a nearby bay to find him with his first 20, a fine 23lb 4oz. What particularly pleased me was that he had managed to land the fish and sack it up on his own. Even though Wayne and I blanked, I went home a happy man. It is also worth noting that he now seems to catch one or two fish per session and recently caught his second 20 at 20lb 8oz.

Over the years then, mates and I have had some good and some bad times fishing the lakes. Apart from the 4/0s in my hand, I have also managed to break my nose while launching my boat. Friends have also had a few encounters with hooks, sometimes even having to moor the boat up and go to the local hospital to remove hooks and have tetanus jabs; but I suppose that it all goes with the territory. Once I remember the engine breaking down on Derwent Water in a big swell and trying to row to the shore. However, the rowlock broke and the wind pushed us down to the other end of the lake. I then had to thumb a lift back to the car with a guy in a two-seater sports car. His dog had to sit on my knee and persisted in licking my face the whole journey back. All in all though, we have thoroughly enjoyed the lakes and the fishing it has to offer, but before concluding I shall provide a brief rundown of some of the main waters. This should be a good starting point for anyone wanting to visit and pike fish in the area.

A Lakeland Tour

Windermere is the largest lake, and, unsurprisingly, being big it has big-fish potential. But it is probably the busiest of the lakes as far as pike fishing goes. I started fishing there in 1997 and at first it was fairly quiet but over recent years it has gained in popularity with people fishing most days, with weekends obviously being the busiest days. It is full of features but it can be a difficult lake to which to gain success. Even when you know this lake well it sometimes seems as if it is totally devoid of fish, and this is where

Young Stevie Hincks with his bank-caught 23lb 4oz.

the use of a boat can come into its own. But if you are going to fish Windermere by boat you will need to register with the National Trust and display a set of numbers on your vessel. There are launch sites on the east and the west shore. If fishing the lake in summer an eye must be kept on the numerous hire boats. These tend to be rowing or small motor boats and they can be a nuisance. Some people seem to be unaware that you are fishing and quite regularly go over lines, no matter how much you try to warn them. Shore fishing can be difficult because many of the banks are privately owned and poor access to good water and overhanging trees can make it difficult to cast. Wading out is not really an option, with lots of areas having steep drop-offs close in. Finally, the official lake record is supposed to be 37lb but I have never seen photographs nor know the name of the captor. The lake certainly has produced fish over 30lb but these are rare creatures indeed.

Coniston is another large lake with shallower and weedier areas in the far north and south, while the central region has very steep sides and deep drop-offs. There are plenty of pike here up to high doubles although 20s are quite rare. The lake's record is a mammoth fish of 38lb 4oz, caught in February 2004. This was a real bolt out of the blue, especially for a lake that does not do many fish over 20lb. As far as I know, there is only one launch site and this is at the north of the lake where there is an annual charge for the combination lock. You can pay to launch daily but you have to wait until the café opens at 9.00 a.m. If you are bank fishing on Coniston there are many easy access points and car parks down the east shore but not so many on the west.

Sandwiched between Windermere and Coniston is Esthwaite Water. This has to be the lake that has produced the most 30lb plus pike in the Lake District, including 35lb-plus specimens

Stephen Hincks with a bank-caught 28lb; note the overhanging trees that can make casting difficult.

such as Dave Lumb's 37lb 6oz on a float-trolled trout livebait in 1993. Boats are available on site for hire and there is good bank access all around the lake. It is a fairly shallow lake in comparison with the rest of the lakes, with maximum depths of around 50ft. Unlike Windermere and Coniston, which are free fishing, day tickets must be bought from the office on the south-west side. There are also privilege access events run through the PAC and the Lure Anglers Club, both being lure only. They usually take place in the spring and the summer, and on the right day good numbers of fish are caught up to high 20s.

Bassenthwaite in the north of the lakes is another generally shallow water with depths to 50ft. As far as I know there is only one slipway and that is half-way up the west side. The lake has produced fish to over 30lb in the past, but these are even more rare than 30s from Windermere. I have heard of only one 30 coming from here, a fish of 32lb from the bank. Lots of jacks and doubles tend to dominate although there is the occasional 20.

Derwent Water, again in the north of the lakes, has depths of up to 70ft. There is a launch site at the southern end of the lake and reasonable access down the west side, with lots of points and bays to fish. The deeper water is down the southern two-thirds of the lake, with the top third being very shallow. The east side has poor parking and access. There are lots of jacks and doubles with 20lb fish rare and 30s unheard of. Derwent Water pike seem to be quite lean in comparison with those from most of the other lakes, despite the fact that there are plenty of prey fish. Overall, this lake is very quiet as regards to pike fishing, and even on a weekend you may be the only one fishing there.

For anyone fancying a challenge, Ullswater in the north east is said to hold no pike whatsoever. It is a very steep-sided, deep lake with few shallow areas with weed beds and the like. However, it is full of small brown trout and perch and these, coupled with no pike-fishing pressure, mean that any resident pike that may or may not be there should be very large. I have

Coniston, scene of a 38lb 4oz fish in 2004, but do not go expecting to catch a 30.

heard stories of people attempting to catch pike, having had some huge fish follow lures, but these are only stories. There are launch sites and reasonable parking down the east and the west side. I have never fished it but good luck to anyone who has a go.

Haweswater is situated in north-east lakeland and, although it is very scenic, being surrounded by steep, rugged fells, it can appear rather daunting. I would say that you should not go expecting to catch on your first visit, but sticking it out could lead to a biggie being caught. Access is easiest on the south bank where the road follows the shoreline.

Wastwater and Ennerdale Water in the west are again very deep and underfished. Surely these waters must contain some pike, so again, with little to no pike-fishing pressure, I would bet that there are one or two biggies waiting to be caught.

Buttermere, Crummock Water and Loweswater share a compact valley in the north west. They are three of the more scenic lakes and all contain pike, although they can be hard to catch. But, they are only lightly fished and, for those who want to fish in solitude in beautiful surroundings, these lakes are hard to beat; do not expect any monsters. The easiest access is from the road that skirts the eastern shore of all the lakes.

Rydal Water and Grasmere just north of Windermere are very similar lakes, both containing pike to around the mid-20s mark, with Grasmere doing genuine 30s in the distant past. There are a few car parks around the lakes and some are close to good fishing spots, but long walks are the order of the day to get to some of the better areas. As far as I know, there is no boat fishing on Rydal, but boats are allowed on Grasmere with a slipway at the north of the lake.

Thirlmere is situated between Ambleside and Keswick. It is a huge water, being some 3½ miles long and 150ft deep at the northern end. Easy access can be had via car parks, particularly along the west side. There is a slipway but powered boats are not allowed. It is probably best not to expect many pike above the 20lb mark.

As indicated earlier, as well as the lakes, other waters such as tarns, canals and rivers should not be overlooked. One of the prettiest and most accessible tarns, for example, is Loughrigg near Skelwith Bridge on the A593, Ambleside–Coniston road. The pike might not be big but the sport can be prolific at times. Less accessible are Burnmoor Tarn, south of Wastwater, and Easedale Tarn, near Grasmere. Both involve some strenuous walking to get to, but if you like lots of action from small pike in isolated surroundings these waters are for you. Then there is the previously mentioned Ulverston Canal, which has lots of pike up to 10lb and even a few 20s, with the three wide basins being as good a place as any to start from. And as for rivers, I recall that when I first joined the Blackpool branch of the PAC, two of the members were catching pike to 25lb plus from a river in the Lake District, which I suspected was the Brathay as it nears Windermere. I must also mention the rivers Eden and Lune, near Carlisle and Lancaster, respectively. Although more renowned for their game fishing, pike are also found in these lower reaches although access can be difficult.

All in all then, I hope that anyone who visits the lakes can make use of this chapter, not least as a rough guide to the pike waters and the pike fishing here. In addition, I sincerely wish you all the best if you decide to have a crack at this beautiful area of the country.

7 NORTHERN ENGLAND RESERVOIR PIKE

Steve Rogowski and Steve Ormrod

Reservoirs are renowned for producing specimen pike to above the 30 and even the 40lb mark. One only has to recall sites such as Bough Beech in Kent, Ardleigh in Essex, Llandegfedd Reservoir in South Wales and Blithfield Reservoir in Staffordshire. All these large reservoirs can produce such big pike, not least because of the stocked trout that they have or did have. But this chapter does not dwell on these waters, rather it is the smaller, at least in many cases, and certainly less prolific ones of the north of England that we deal with. There are reservoirs in the north east such as Fontburn Reservoir in Northumberland and Derwent Reservoir in Durham, and there is Killington Reservoir adjacent to Cumbria and the Lake District. All these can produce pike. But here we concentrate on those around Greater Manchester and the Lancashire–Yorkshire borders. They were built in Victorian times not only to provide drinking water but also water for the many canals that dissect the area. This is where we have pike fished regularly over recent years with some success. Although you are unlikely to catch a pike in the 40lb bracket and 30s are certainly hard to achieve, a 20lb-plus specimen is always a possibility.

Piking on a bleak, northern reservoir can be disheartening as there may be acres of featureless water, with the result that you often feel that your baits might not be anywhere near any pike at all. Easy piking is not often found and thus this is not for the faint hearted. But the peace and the space are also reasons why many enjoy such places, and this is why many, including ourselves, often spend cold, wet, windy and generally miserable winter days on them. Indeed, as we write one of us has just spent a gale-lashed day on one. At one stage the sky suddenly darkened and a sort of roaring noise gradually became louder. At first, thoughts turned to its being a low-flying aircraft bound for Manchester Airport, but it was the wind as it picked up even more, as did the rain. Even though it was a very sheltered swim, within a minute or two there were 3ft-high waves crashing into the bank and the umbrella gave way. It really was quite a scary experience, albeit it all ended as suddenly as it started. As for the piking, all that occurred was a dropped run.

As with all attempts at catching pike, persistence and the spending of time and effort mean that success can be gained. Furthermore, it must also be remembered that, although such reservoirs can be little more than concrete bowls, or at best rather boring and featureless, there is often more to this. For instance, Barrowford Reservoir near Colne is certainly one of these bowls, and Mixenden Reservoir near Denholme is also rather less than picturesque. But others, and even parts of these bowls or featureless waters, can be quite scenic and attractive. Combs Reservoir near Chapel-en-le-Frith readily springs to mind here. It is over 57 acres and set in the hills that form the beautiful Peak District of Derbyshire. Lots of pike up to the mid-double mark can be had from here. Although it is readily reached from Manchester and Sheffield, when you are piking here on a warm, sunny spring day, such cities seem far away indeed. Similarly, the top Whiteheads Reservoir near Bury is set in almost equally delightful surroundings consisting of green, rolling hills and gorse bushes, all of which look particularly scenic in the spring. Foulridge Reservoir, Colne and Rakes Brook Reservoir near Darwen are others that are set in quite picturesque surroundings and, furthermore, they can produce pike to well over the 20lb mark.

Not always boring and featureless – a winter sunset on a northern reservoir.

This chapter is divided into two: Steve R. begins by discussing in general terms what can lead to success on these daunting waters, and, in particular, locations, rigs and tactics, including baits. Steve O. then discusses how to tackle a northern reservoir for the first time and highlights the methods that have been productive for him. There is an element of overlap between them and even slight differences of opinion, but these should not come as a surprise since, of course, pike anglers can be very opinionated.

Location, Rigs, Tactics and Baits

Many readers will be aware that reservoirs generally consist of a deep, main body of water averaging 30ft or more, the deepest water usually being off the dam wall and the shallowest being at the opposite end and in the bays and arms. Doe Park Reservoir, for example, at Denholme is a typical tooth-shaped, Pennine reservoir. It is some 20-plus acres in area and said to have some very big pike. One book I read claimed, for example, that 'a dead bait laid well out in the deeper water [presumably near the dam wall] should attract one of these old fish'. But, unfortunately, after several visits I have yet to catch a pike here.

Reservoirs are usually formed by damming rivers or streams, and the original bed or beds will remain as one or more trenches or channels, perhaps joined by subsidiary trenches, channels and streams. There may also be the remains of old buildings and those that have disintegrated into piles of rubble, together with the remains of trees. Good examples are Watergrove Reservoir, Rochdale and Jumbles Reservoir, Bolton. Valve towers and old pump houses are also to be found and perhaps there will also be overhanging bushes and trees and bay areas of weeds and reeds. Examples of these are to be found at Elton Reservoir, Bury and Ogden Reservoir, Rochdale. All such features help to break up the uniform, even boring, aspects of these reservoirs. Although some will be discovered only by looking at old maps or talking to older locals, others can simply be seen. The point is, however, that all these features are potential pike-holding areas. For example, the trenches and channels are where drop-offs and hence pike are to be found, and areas around valve towers and pump houses are attractive to prey fish because of the algae that grow there, which they eat, and the pike will not be far behind. One such pump house provided a great day's sport, at least in terms of the number of pike caught.

The reservoir in question is not in a picturesque setting, surrounded as it is by the sight and sounds of metro-trains, houses, factories and even, believe it or not, a dilapidated nightclub. But the piking can be good, with fish to the double-figure mark being common. I arrived soon after dawn on the day in question. It was a cloudy, mild October day. Mist was slowly clearing from the water and, after disturbing several ducks and swans, I quickly put out float and sunken float paternostered and ledgered deadbaits. In the next three hours I had ten runs, resulting in seven pike. Admittedly, they were not massive, with only the biggest two

being near doubles, but that did not detract from the lively and thoroughly enjoyable action, and although the runs slowed down and I started to run out of bait, livebaits were eventually caught and I went on to catch five more pike, even though again they were little more than jacks. But it was still a total of twelve pike in a day, a feat I have equalled only on Yorkshire's River Ouse and Scotland's Loch Ken.

Bigger pike, to over the 20lb mark, are to be had from another reservoir that features flooded, old buildings and piles of rubble. The piking is often slow but it is usual to get one a run or two, commonly to the same ledgered deadbait rod cast into deep water about 30yd from the bank. For example, one cold, though bright and sunny January day led to a fine sixteen pounder succumbing to a ledgered mackerel tail. Such success was obviously welcome despite the fact that

A nicely marked 'scraper' 20 for Steve Rogowski; it seized a float-paternostered live roach cast into deep water alongside bushes.

quite often I used to get snagged, losing tackle in the process. It was only after several visits that an old chap told me that I was fishing where there used to be an old cottage. So, without realizing it, I had actually been casting to a feature and so, with hindsight, it was not really surprising that I usually caught. As we have noted, casting to features often tends to catch pike.

The shallow bays and arms of reservoirs often produce in spring since the pike are likely to be there for spawning. In particular, one bay I know features a small inlet that flows from a trout reservoir further up the valley. This inlet or channel attracts a lot of small roach and perch and from February–March onwards until September pike are regularly to be had. At first they are only jacks and there can be lots of them, but you also have the chance of a large female. In fact, this is the area where I have had most of my reservoir 20s even though they have usually tended to be 'scrapers' just over the 20lb mark. One I particularly recall was caught in July. I arrived at mid morning after having had a pint or two too many the night before. Sunken float paternoster and ledgered dead roach were cast out. Within minutes I had begun catching roach and quickly swapped a dead for a live on the sunken paternoster. This was cast about a rod length out beside a bush into about 10ft of water. Not long after, the bite alarm and dropback were triggered and I struck home into what I immediately knew was a nice fish. The rod was bent solid for a time before, after a lively scrap, she eventually came to the net and was weighed in at exactly 20lb.

Into the autumn and winter the deeper water off dam walls is well worth a try. Pike tend retreat here at such times of the year, probably because these areas offer a degree of temperature and disturbance stability. Admittedly, they then spend long periods where they are inactive, during which time their heart rate and bodily functions slow down, including feeding. But they can still be caught. During one December near a dam wall I repeatedly seemed to have a run or two and catch even though I was doing only short afternoon sessions. Once I arrived at 1.0 p.m. on a cloudy, chilly but dry day, with a brisk south-westerly wind. I cast out three rods with ledgered mackerel head and tails. A little over half an hour later the alarm with one of the tails went off and I was soon into a solid tussle with a large pike. At first there was nothing frantic about the runs but they oozed a sort of deep, quiet, ominous power. A minute or two later the pike neared the surface with gills flared, maw gaping and white water flying everywhere. On first seeing her massive head I thought it might be a first 30. She surged away again, doing this several times, before I managed to scoop her into the net. She was a large, magnificent pike and the weighing revealed her to be a 27lb 8oz specimen. My heart was pumping, not least because she was (and remains) my second personal best. The photographs were quickly taken by a friendly fellow piker further along the bank. He was very impressed to see what was his biggest ever pike, but he was shaking with excitement so much that only one picture came out. Nevertheless, what was also very satisfying about this capture was that the bailiff went on to say that she was the biggest pike to come out of that water in the last few years. And, who knows, she could well have been a 30 some three months or so later before she spawned.

The following December I went back to the same swim in the hope of catching this thirty pounder. In fact, ten sessions took place, but all I had to show for this effort was a hesitant, dropped run. Part of the explanation for my lack of success when compared to the previous year's no doubt related to the fact that the reservoir was now full whereas before it had been some 12ft lower after the long, hot summer of 2003.

In any case, as suggested, the point has to be made that reservoirs can be very slow in cold weather. The pike seem to disappear, but in reality they are likely to gather up, not appearing to feed, only renewing their enthusiasm when the weather breaks. In fact, Danny Haynes, an experienced reservoir piker from the north west of England, once had fourteen consecutive blanks during a winter campaign on one of these hard waters. These periods would make even worse reading were it not for a 5lb jack that broke up

A plump reservoir 27lb 8oz fish for Steve Rogowski, which fell to a ledgered half mackerel. A pity that only one photograph came out.

Danny Haynes with a twenty-two pounder that took a fancy to a ledgered deadbait.

the blanking sessions. But despite the blanks, Danny tends to emphasize the pleasures to be gained from northern reservoir piking. There is the tranquillity to be gleaned from relaxing in, as can often be found, nice scenery, perhaps observing the birds, which can vary from small blue tits and robins to large Canada geese. Even watching the dreaded cormorants can break up the day. Then there is the other wildlife, which can include shrews, squirrels and foxes. And, not least, there is always a chance of a large pike. He well recalls a memorable week one November a few years ago.

At the time he was arriving at his swim mid morning and setting up two rods. The swim itself consisted of a small, bay-like area surrounded by bushes that provided shelter from the more severe weather. On this particular day though it was quite bright and mild, with only a slight ripple on the water. The left-hand rod featured a ledgered herring 'gently lobbed out' to a 'gravel bar-type' feature. The right-hand rod had a ledgered mackerel tail 'punched out' some 60yd over a slow drop-off towards the middle of the reservoir. After a couple of hours, the alarm on the left rod 'went ballistic' and he wound down into what he immediately knew was a solid fish. She initially powered to the left and then to the right before coming to the net. The weighing revealed her to be 18lb exactly. It was to be the only run of the day, but, nonetheless, was very welcome for that.

Three days later Danny arrived at the swim at more or less the same time. On this occasion it was more of an overcast day and there was a stronger ripple on the water. The same two rods were cast to the same features, with joey herring and joey mackerel on the left- and right-hand rods, respectively. Shortly afterwards it was the herring that went producing a slow but steady run, followed by a hard tussle that eventually led to another fine 18lb fish being banked. To begin with he thought that it was the same pike as previously, but a slight blemish in her tail meant that it was a different fish. He really was 'chuffed to bits', two high doubles in the same week on a hard water was pretty good piking. And then,

late in the afternoon in low light conditions with slight drizzle, his right-hand alarm 'zipped off'. On striking home, the fish hugged the bottom and powered off to the right. After several minutes she tired and slowly came to the net, with the weighing scales showing her to be 21lb 8oz. After several years of trying it was his first 20 at the venue and so a photograph was obviously needed. He quickly telephoned the bailiff, who kindly came and did the honours.

Moving to rigs and tactics, I have already indicated the rigs that I generally favour – float and sunken float paternoster and ledger. On arriving at my chosen swim I also like to cast out a baited rod immediately, usually a ledgered deadbait, before setting up the rest of my tackle. (You will probably be surprised at how often a run seems to ensue while you are busy sorting out the rest of your gear.)

Although I have referred to the set ups that I usually use, it must be remembered that pike are not always near the bottom and so it is often worthwhile fishing baits higher in the water. For instance, in the first decades after the Second World War pikers, including my dad and his friend, often used large bungs with baits only 4 or 5ft underneath and they often caught. Thus, using a simple float rig, with greased line if casting any distance, can bring success with both live and deadbaits, as can drifting, albeit I have not tried this method often enough. I do not want to sound too technical, but success with such methods is especially likely when the water stratifies, usually in summer, into layers: there is the warmer, upper layer (the epilimnion), followed by the middle layer (the thermocline) and then there is the bottom layer (the hypolimnion). Such a condition can lead to the thermocline's producing, this possibly having something to do with the fact that there is a 'sandwich' of rapidly changing temperature.

On a different tack, piking into the wind can be productive. Many pikers often swear that you need 'a bit of a ripple on the water', ideally from a south-west direction, in order to catch. It must also be remembered that the northern reservoirs that I am describing are susceptible to winds, and very strong ones at that (see Steve O.'s comments below). Such a situation means that the warmer, upper layer of water is pushed to the bank, while waves into the shoreline also push more dissolved oxygen into the water. Prey fish are often attracted and hence pike.

As for casting, it may be stating the obvious, but there is no need to cast to the horizon with a 3 or 4oz bomb and then back-wind. No doubt this will catch pike and it may look and feel rather macho, but in my experience distance casting is not always necessary. The base of the near shelf is often the place to be. As well as the 'scraper' 20 referred to above, I well recall catching many other 'scraper' 20s some 3 or 4yd from the bank on float and sunken float paternoster rigs. It goes without saying that this is often the place for most of the fish, and the pike will not be far behind.

Pre-baiting is often advocated as a good method of attracting pike to particular swims when you are faced with large, difficult waters. No doubt this has worked for many although I have to admit that when I first tried this it seemed to have little effect. In fact, I recall pre-baiting an area over a two-week period and felt confident as I set up two ledgered mackerel tail rods together with a sunken paternostered dead roach. I had arrived soon after dawn, but by mid afternoon the rods remained untouched. I decided to move one ledgered rod to an adjacent swim and cast a couple of rod lengths out over a sharp drop-off. Sure enough, within minutes the alarm screeched away and I was into a pike which turned out to be a nice double.

However, there is no doubt that pre-baiting can draw pike to a

Steve Rogowski with a recent reservoir mid-double caught on a ledgered half jack.

particular area. Big pike are often very lazy so, when they find an easy meal, they will not turn it down and, once they find it, they are likely to be back for more. Pre-baiting can also keep pike healthy and increase their confidence in feeding. But you have to find the right swim, for example, one that has produced pike before but is not so popular that it could mean someone else benefitting from all your pre-baiting work. The swim should also be not far from home and accessible, with a feature such as a drop-off or overhanging trees and bushes. And what about the pre-bait itself? Every winter I tend to clear out my deadbaits, not least looking for previously used baits that I have saved. They are then defrosted overnight before they are introduced into the chosen swim on, say, alternate days. About 1lb of bait is used each time and then, after a couple of weeks or so, the swim should be ready to be fished with the types of bait you have been pre-baiting with. If you get things right, a big pike can be the reward.

Turning more specifically to baits, I guess that initially one must try equally hard with live and with deadbaits. The latter, especially on a hard water, need to be fresh, although you can get away with using refrozen baits on easier waters. In any case, you will probably find the seasonal nature in the way that bait preferences reveal themselves – broadly, lives in summer and deads in winter. However, of course, this is not always the case and, conversely, you can catch on livebaits in winter and deadbaits in summer. I have caught 20s on, for example, a dead jack and a mackerel head in summer. And it is also worth commenting on the view that you will generally catch larger pike on deadbaits. In my experience, it is about 50–50 as regards deadbaits and livebaits in catching the 'biggies'. On one particular reservoir it seems to be that live roach lead to success especially in the warmer months; this probably has something to do with the fact that they are the predominant prey fish in this water.

What about favourite baits? As usual, you cannot be too dogmatic and, in any case, there is no magic bait as such. In my view, it pays to experiment constantly, not least because the exception often proves the rule. But if I do have any favourite baits then, as far as lives are concerned, roach (again) and perch should be mentioned. As for deads, mackerel head and tail seem to be the baits that have provided the most regular successes. Such half baits are obviously of a smaller size than whole baits, this means that you can strike instantly, confident that the hooks are in the pike's mouth. Also remember that the juices flow freely out of the bait, which attract pike. It goes without saying that deads such as smelt, herring and lamprey also have their days, as do dead coarse fish generally, but, in my experience, especially dead gudgeon.

How to Tackle a Northern Reservoir for the First Time

So, Steve Rogowski has looked in general terms at pike fishing on these waters, but how do we go about tackling one of these northern reservoirs for the first time? A first bit of advice is: do not be tempted simply to turn up and fish them. There are several reasons for saying this: first, you need to gain proper permission to do so and purchase the appropriate club card or day ticket in advance; secondly, you may not have a clue about where to start or gain access and you will waste valuable fishing time; and thirdly, you could end by not having the right gear to fish the water successfully.

If possible, I advise you to visit the venue in midsummer, before the forthcoming winter season. I would wait for a really dry spell and then go, have a good look and make notes. The water levels will be well down and many features, not least the drop-offs, will be high and dry. It is also worthwhile taking a camera along to take sufficient photographs, since these will prove priceless when the waters rise.

In the autumn and early winter I would then have a half-day recce, but do not go dressed in your best fishing-branded fleece since the more you look like a walker or a member of the general public the better. Taking the all-important

A basic selection of lures, including, for example, spoons and crankbaits.

RIGHT: Karl 'King of the Jacks' Highton, this time with a reservoir double. It was caught on a sunken paternostered live roach cast to a 10ft-deep inlet to a northern reservoir.

BELOW: The rods are in at dawn on Esthwaite.

A 17lb 8oz canal pike for Steve Rogowski, which fell to a float-ledgered herring head cast into a shallow inlet.

John Sadd with his 'back-end' Horsey Mere fish, weighing 30lb 10oz.

Dick Culpin's youngest son Tom, with his first double.

Jason Davies with a magnificent 37lb 4oz from Blithfield.

Nige Williams with his Blithfield 32lb 6oz.

Battered Springdawgs, which did so well at Ladybower in the early days. Note that one has lost the tip, but these are easily replaced.

Beautiful, clean and fat – not Neville Fickling but the pike.

RIGHT: Richard Young with a River Aire double, which succumbed to ledgered half mackerel cast to overhanging bushes on the far bank.

An early Ure double for Steve Rogowski, caught on a ledgered sprat cast into a deeper channel.

Darren Lord with his 29lb14oz Esthwaite fish.

Eric 'The Fish' Brown with a cracking personal best 24lb 12oz (photograph: courtesy of Eric Brown).

Steve Ormrod and a lean, mean, summer-caught 21lb fish.

This 16lb 8oz was caught on a sunken paternostered live roach by Steve Rogowski.

Bill Palmer with a superb 33lb 12oz gravel-pit pike.

ABOVE: *Bernard Palmer with an Ardleigh 20.*

RIGHT: *Mick Toomer with the Warren monster before she went to the taxidermist's.*

BELOW: *A chunky 32lb 8oz for Andrew Gallagher from a Welsh still water.*

ABOVE: Scottish pike fishing can be excellent and the scenery is not bad either, as this photograph of a moody Loch Arkaig shows.

RIGHT: Steve Ormrod's piking partner Graham Barstow, with a cracking Loch Oich 21s.

BELOW: This 28lb 14oz beauty was caught in May by Mark Ackerley from Lough Mask on a wobbled deadbait.

camera and binoculars, the best time to go will be 10a.m. on a Sunday morning. Plan to have a couple of hours mooching until lunchtime. One may well ask, why be so specific about all of this? The answer is that, if the water has pike potential, there will be pike anglers around and you will be able to see what they are up to. Sunday is the main fishing day for most of them, hence this is the best day to go. Such anglers can be a secretive bunch, especially if they think you are a potential competitor, thus an element of disguise. By turning up mid morning the anglers present will have been fishing for a few hours and, if you chat like an interested spectator, you may well get some useful information. But beware: mention that you are an angler only if it seems appropriate, otherwise the angler you speak to may well clam up on you. It is also a good idea to offer some information yourself, quid pro quo, but not the location of your banker waters, of course.

You should also stroll round the reservoir more generally, taking note of any interesting swims and visible features. Are there swims being fished by anglers and, if so, ask yourself why? After all, they will not be fishing there without a reason. Try to have a chat as just described and find out all you can, such as the piking potential, the history of the water and tickets. Also note how the angler is fishing and any baits he may be using. Is the unhooking mat or landing net wet or slimy? Is there a weigh-sling hanging to dry? This might all sound a little devious, but any information gained will aid you in quickly getting to grips with the place and, believe me, you will need it for starters.

You should also take note of the prevailing wind direction. Even though it may be calm you can still see evidence if you look carefully at the trees, for instance. In which direction are some of them bent over? The clues are all there, if you are prepared to look. Where does the sun rise and fall? This may affect when you will fish certain swims because, for example, if it is a bright day they may fish better before or after the sun has been on them. Look at the bankside, will banksticks suffice or do you need to use a pod?

You will need a pod on the dam wall I can assure you. Are the swims a long walk away from the car? If so, you can tackle down to suit. Take lots of reference pictures and use the binoculars to look at far-off areas first before tramping round and finding them inaccessible. It is all about preparation and the alleviation of any obvious problems before you start to fish.

Having heeded the above you should have a clearer picture of what is what, and then you will have probably decided to give the water a go. Even so, the vastness of reservoirs might put you off, but even this can be alleviated if you follow the next few tips. First, make a drawing of the water from an Ordnance Survey map and write on where the compass points are. Then indicate the prevailing wind directions and mark on the potential swims discovered from the recce, also mark on the dam wall and any landmarks, noting that high banks that run into the water will probably indicate deep water below as the steepness continues. Similarly, gently sloping banks probably indicate shallows. Make a rough indication of where you suspect these deep and shallow areas exist and mark any arms, gullies and inlet streams, and, indeed, any features that break up the reservoir. In effect, you are now looking at several smaller waters. This should begin to make you feel more in control, confident and almost ready to start fishing. I say almost ready because, if you are keen enough, a second pre-fishing visit is also worthwhile before the serious stuff starts. On that second visit take both plumbing and lure rods with you and visit the favoured areas you have earmarked. Use a large, highly visible float and a 3oz lead on your plumbing gear since you first want to cast some distance. As for lures, take a selection of your bankers.

Correctly plumbing the swims is probably the most important exercise as it enables you to build up a picture of what is there. You may already have a rough idea from the summer visit and you will have the pictures to compare with the now full reservoir, but it also pays to know the exact depths too. My approach is to do a series of 'fan-casts' with the rig in an arc from right to left of the swim if possible. Cast well out so that you can see where the deeper water lies, retrieving the rig and taking depth readings as it nears the bank side. Take note of your findings and try to figure out if there are any humps, gullies, sandbars, shelves, drop-offs and the like. Also take note of how far out they are too. This saves precious time when you come to fish the swim as you will know exactly where to cast. It will also prevent you from disturbing the swim too much.

After plumbing it is time for some fun and possible reward for your efforts by having a cast around with the lures to see whether you get any interest. If you do, you will have an even better idea of where to start your campaign by having your first proper piking trip.

It may be stating the obvious, but you will need to take a selection of deadbaits that are allowed on the water concerned. For instance, some waters do not allow coarse deadbaits because of the risk of illegal livebaiting. If you want to livebait (if it is allowed, of course) then bring a rod and bait and catch them at the venue, although you may find northern reservoirs difficult. Personally, I do not bother unless they are easy to catch and prove to be more successful than deadbaits in sorting out the better fish. In my experience on these waters deads always catch the bigger pike. I would give it a full day's fishing to start with by going before dawn, choosing a swim and sticking with it until dusk. In this way you will build up a picture of the swim, both in terms of finding features and actually catching pike. By repeating this in several swims you will soon find out whether each one is a 'dawn', 'morning', 'midday', 'afternoon' or a

Steve Ormrod carefully returning a 22lb 12oz to her reservoir home.

'dusk' swim. They are likely to produce in just one or two of these periods and only rarely in all five.

You should arrive stealthily at the swim, drop the gear well away from the water and set up quietly. Make sure that you wear dark or camouflage gear in order to blend in and creep up to the water, keeping a low profile. Push rather than hammer the banksticks, in thereby not disturbing any pike that may be present. Normally you can fish a maximum of four rods on these waters, but make sure that you have two licences if you are fishing more than two rods. I find that three rods are more than enough, especially if the fish are feeding. My tactics vary, but I would start off with one rod set up for margin-ledgering, either with a light bomb or a small float-ledger set-up. It is certainly important not to discount the near margins, especially if there is a decent depth of 6ft. This can be a banker tactic and I have caught dozens of big 20s using it. It is amazing how big fish will come in so close, especially when you look out on to the vast area of water and consider what features must be out there.

Margin fishing can work in swims where there are overhanging or semi-submerged trees and bushes on either side of the swim, since the pike like to come close in and patrol round these features. But do not discount open water areas, especially if there is a feature such a gully close in or by a stream inlet. Gently lob your bait in a few yards, say five or six, and have some defrosted and chopped-up baits with you and throw them in around your bait. I would then be tempted to sit back, have a hot drink and keep quiet for an hour to see whether there are any feeding pike in

Almost a 30 for Steve Ormrod at 29lb 12oz. It was the best of three 20s caught in one morning.

your immediate vicinity. If so they will soon show themselves. I know that you are fishing only one rod, but it may prove a success. If it does, then you could always fish all three rods similarly since you may have tempted the fish to feed close in. I have taken a 200lb-plus bag of pike, including a near 30 and two decent 20s in one day by using this method. But having said that, if it is still quiet after an hour then get the other two rods in.

I normally set the second rod up for float ledgering and, by doing this, you can see what sort of depth you are fishing as compared with what your initial plumbing indicated. For instance, you may well want to fish a sandbar that you found; it is 12ft deep on the top with drop-offs to 20ft on either side and it is 30yd out, in line with a tall pine tree on the far bank. By setting your stop-knot to 13ft you will soon find it; either the unbaited rig will disappear into the deeps or the float will lie flat on the bar because the rig is slightly over-depth. Give it another twitch and it should disappear again over the near side. With practice and a few trips you will know exactly where to cast to first go. It is a good feature to try because the pike will patrol along the shelves and over the sandbar itself. Please do not use loaded pencil floats for this style of piking since they will lead to deep-hooked fish. Use the unloaded version that 'cocks' as you tighten the line to the bobbin.

Other key areas include the gullies between the silt humps that accumulate on these waters. Pike will move into them to have a mooch around, especially if the weather is rough because they provide shelter from the chop and the undertow. This is where having seen the summer low levels comes into its own – you will have seen all the humps and gullies and recorded their positions for the winter. A useful tip if you are in a tight swim is that by using the float-ledger set-up on your middle rod you will be able to play any fish on the right or the left rod under the line of this rod as the line will be near the surface because of the float. This can be a life-saver at times.

As for the third rod, I would definitely use a sunken float paternoster; it has caught so many

reservoir pike for me that I have lost count. The good thing about using a suspended deadbait is that you are utilizing the undertow, which is present more often than not. By using a large, fat, sunken float some movement will be given to the deadbait as it wobbles in the current. Takes are absolute screamers since the pike thinks that the deadbait is a dying prey item struggling to swim. I have noticed that it is very successful in windy conditions where the wave action and the undertow are especially strong. I fish this rig at middle distance on features such drop-offs and shelves to make the best use of the wave and the undertow action. Perhaps surprisingly, half sardines cut at an angle have been very good at producing. I also use this rig with large 2oz feeders filled with mashed sardine, this replaces the lead as a casting weight and serves as a localized attractant.

Having looked at the main methods I prefer, it is worth commenting on some other useful hints and tips, beginning with 'twitching'. I sometimes twitch a deadbait by reeling in a few yards every half-hour or so while float ledgering. It is amazing how it can instigate an immediate take as a pike may have been been eyeing it for some time, but that bit of movement can make all the difference. But do be careful if you are fishing a boulder-strewn bed since you will soon snag-up. Try and incorporate weak links in your rigs so that bombs pull away easily if snagged. Strong braid will allow you to straighten out hooks too. Next, sink and draw can be a deadly method if you are facing a blank with the usual methods. I use a shorter rod for this, but any decent, 12ft pike rod will still do the job. I like to hook up a perch in a curve, add a few swan-shot and lightly flick the bait along the margins to sunken trees or along the dam wall edge. Let it sink and then slowly retrieve it, letting it flutter down now and again. The curve in the bait makes it 'wobble' enticingly and the secret is in the slow retrieval and letting it settle now and again. As soon as you get a hit treat it like a normal run. It can be great fun and sometimes guarantees a bonus fish. Thirdly, although I am not really a lure man, I like having a go now and then. Summer is a great time to get on these waters with the lures, especially when levels are low too. Most patterns and lure types work so that all I can suggest is to try with your banker lures. Fourthly, livebaiting is not something I do much these days for the reasons mentioned earlier. However, they can be productive so long as you fish them where the better fish are expected to be since nine times out of ten you will be troubled by the jacks. One great tactic I have used is to fish a 'straight-line' lure by your tethered livebaits. I cast well past where the livebait is fishing and retrieve the lure past it. Often you will get a take on the livebait as a pike has followed the

lure and then spotted an easier target. Fifthly, distance ledgering is a good tactic that is venue-dependent. Some reservoirs have features a long way out, a sunken stream inlet, for instance. With a good casting technique and using a decent 13ft distance rod and big-spooled reel, simple rigs, big leads and an aerodynamic bait like half a launce, you should be able to hit 100yd. One reservoir I used to fish had large buoys anchored some 80yd out and it always proved to be a hotspot as the prey fish would be feeding on algae gathered on the buoy ropes. Sixthly, drifting can bring success although this

A young Neil Macdonald proudly shows off his winter-caught 15lb 8oz.

takes some patience to get to grips with on big reservoirs. Certain swims will be impossible to master due to the undertow and the lie of the land behind you, and northern reservoirs are often in hilly areas that funnel the wind and send it swirling all over the water, not necessarily in the same direction. However, if you get some level land behind you and a good blow then some exciting drifts can be achieved. And finally a comment about baitboats. These can be useful to get to difficult swims, but use them sensibly and do not place baits in swims that look snaggy or where you are unaware what lies between you and the end rig.

Before concluding it is important to emphasize that weather plays a big part in terms of success or otherwise on northern reservoirs. Most of the time you will have the threat of big winds and driving rain to cope with, the sky draped in endless, grey blankets. In fact, the wind plays a big part in the choice of swim for me. Very rarely will I not bother to go if a certain wind is blowing, but I find the southerly and the westerly winds are the best and I try to fish a swim with a cross-wind in preference to 'full-on'. However, get a warm spell with a moderate southerly in the middle of a cold snap and it pays to fish the windward bank since it will be warmer there. Even easterly winds do not put me off, even if it can be really cold with temperatures below freezing point if you add in the chill factor. What I do in these conditions is fish the east bank in a sheltered spot, say under some trees, noting that the fish will often come there for sanctuary out of the main blow too.

In general, I can usually land on some fish, knowing, from my records and notes, that I will be there at a favourable time, in the right swim, fishing the right features and with the winning tactics and baits. Incidentally, mentioning the last, my favourites are sardines (full and halved), joey mackerel, halved large mackerel, lamprey and launce halves, smelts and, where allowed, roach, rudd and perch. I have tried exotics and the like but I always come back to these bankers.

In concluding then, we hope that we have provided you with some incentive to give northern reservoirs a try. Although the piking can be difficult, equally there are rewards to be had with some good fish to be caught. One particular plus with these waters is the 'unknown factor'. This is the fact that you can catch a large pike, one you have never seen before, despite having fished the place extensively for some time. It really can be a big bonus. If you persevere then, you will gain experience, knowledge and eventually land a few fish, and a picture of the water will naturally unfold. This is especially so if you keep careful records and notes of your visits – the dates, fishing times, conditions, methods and baits and catches. For example, one of us has a favourite venue that started with several blank sessions. But to date it has now led to the capture of many doubles and 20s near to the 30lb mark. Such comparisons will leave you wondering whether you are fishing the same water. As with a lot of fishing, it is not all black and white, but time, patience and the resulting experience will eventually lead to success.

8 PIKE FISHING IN THE SOUTH EAST OF ENGLAND

Bill Palmer

Most types of pike fishing water are catered for in the south east of England. For example, river piking can be had along many stretches of the mighty Thames, in Surrey there is the River Wey, which flows into the Thames at Weybridge, in Sussex there are the rivers Arun and Adur. There is also the River Lea, which flows through Hertfordshire to London. In Kent we have the Medway, which flows to the Thames estuary at Sheerness, the Rother, which rises at Rotherfield and enters the sea at Rye and the Stour, which rises near Ashford and flows to the coast near Sandwich. Apart from these rivers, there is also canal piking to be had in other waters, not least from the numerous canals that criss-cross much of London. Finally, but certainly not least, there are the still-waters of ponds, lakes, reservoirs and gravel pits, which can be a pike angler's dream.

Although I fished with some success on the Stour at places such as Grove Ferry and Plucks Gutter, it was some years ago. My river fishing these days takes place on the Waveney in Suffolk and the Yare in Norfolk. My piking partner Steve Wells and I have had stacks of doubles and a number of 20s to just under 29lb. Such waters are covered elsewhere in this book and so I shall not dwell on them here. Instead, this chapter deals with some of the main reservoirs, lakes and gravel pits of the south east, since, after all, over the years I have spent much of my spare time fishing for pike on such waters. Although pike fishing here can be challenging at times, on the other hand there are some very big fish to be had.

At the outset I hope that the reader will understand if I do not name nor provide precise details of all of the waters I fish. I do not want to be unduly secretive but there are a large number of pike anglers in this area of the country and I do not want to tread on the toes of those already fishing here. To name such waters is likely to put extra pressure on them and, in turn, the pike, something I want to try and avoid. I cannot do much about the already well known and publicized waters and so I shall not be giving much away when I refer to them. But, having got this off my chest, let us have a look at what the south east can offer the pike angler.

I was born and brought up in this area of the country and most of my early pike fishing was done around Essex and Hertfordshire lakes and gravel pits. My very first pike were caught from the ornamental waters in Wanstead Park in east London. They were 12in monsters, which were taken on small livebaits when I was a very small boy. In my teens I progressed to the big gravel pits in the Lea Valley around Cheshunt, catching my first doubles out of the North Metropolitan Police Pit. Now, fifty years on, I travel a lot further afield for most of my piking, but since I still live in Essex, it is the reservoirs, lakes and gravel pits of the south east that are my local waters. In this chapter I shall first deal with reservoirs, then lakes and gravel pits, and, before concluding, briefly consider methods, rigs and baits.

Reservoirs

Let us begin with the non-trout reservoirs, and the first I was to fish was the King George V at Ponders End, north London. It was some forty odd years ago and a workmate Bob Slaughter and I had three mid-doubles on our first session. What a start it was, and so began my love affair with the big reservoir at Ponders End, one that was to last five years.

Jeff Ducker with a mid-20 from the King George V Reservoir in the late 1970s.

The King George V had 5 miles of bank with depths averaging over 20ft. Although it was one of the best kept secrets, in the early 1970s it must have been one of the best pike waters in the south east. Fishing with my good friends Len Savage, Jeff Ducker and Colin Benbrook we came up with a lot of rigs that I still use to the present. For example, we used air-injected deadbaits, poly-balled livebait rigs, dead and livebait rigs and the slow sinker. Although any bait and any method will always catch pike, I maintain that to achieve consistently good results you need to be versatile, constantly trying something new. The aforementioned rigs were all developed and subsequently refined, all those years ago.

During our first season on the George I caught twenty or so pike, the average weight being 18lb 4oz. My mates had similar success, with Len keeping a record on the back of one of his cigarette packets of all the pike caught. He then transferred it to his diary when he got home, pointing out that, on average, every third fish was a 20. It was just like being in heaven. After struggling to

catch, say, ten doubles a season, I was in with a real chance of ten 20s. And it was on the George all those years ago that I was to land my most 20s in a day – four up to 26lb 2oz, plus a 19lb 8oz, for a total weight of 115lb. Although I have caught three 20s in a day another seven times, it is perhaps unsurprising that I have not been able to beat that day. It really was a great place to pike fish.

In just five short years we saw well over a hundred 20s caught, my personal tally being about thirty. Apart from the capture of big pike, I loved the freedom there, being able to fish how I wanted, to use what bait I chose and being able to put out another rod without looking over my shoulder. I was fishing with good friends with whom you could always have a laugh and a joke, and we were responsible anglers who did not abuse our freedom. Because of all this there is now a sense of regret that I have not fished the reservoir for many years, and it was sad to hear that it was stocked with carp a few years ago. Then, to cap it all, the last I heard was that the carp had been netted and the reservoir was being drained.

A mention now needs to be made about the Walthamstow group of reservoirs, which are still capable of producing some good pike even though I have not fished them for some thirty years. However, I did catch a 20 from Lockwood Reservoir there in the 1970s, the scene of Roy Whithall's alleged, and subsequently doubted, 43lb 12oz capture. It should also be noted that unfortunately these reservoirs are now mainly carp waters.

The early 1970s also saw my first visit to Abberton Reservoir, near Colchester, and I am still fishing there to this day. It is a very big reservoir and I do mean big, with over 1,000 acres of water and 15 miles of bank, but it is important to note that you are allowed access to fish on only a few hundred yards. When I first fished there you had to buy a ticket before entering, but at £2 a day it was certainly good value, as it still was when tickets gradually went up in price to £5.

One good thing was that livebaiting was allowed as long as it came from the water, and obtaining them was no problem at all. All you had to do was run your landing net along the culvert wall or use a drop net, often you had to let half the fish out so that you could lift the net and you would still have enough for a dozen sessions. It was all so easy, not least the piking itself. There would be lots of runs, some nice doubles and the odd 20. There was no pressure at all and it was a great place to be even though all this was about to change. Today the water company has banned livebaiting and allows deadbaiting only with sea deads. It has also restricted the use of baitboats and turned the place into a £100 per annum season-ticket water, and the best (or worst) of it all is that they have stopped the fishing on the road bank at the small end, thereby cutting in half the few hundred of yards of fishing we had (have you ever felt that you were not wanted?). Be all that as it may, let us get back to the good old days at Abberton.

In 1981 Vic Gibson and Eddie Turner had been experimenting with large, vaned floats. They were certainly different since they had a long stem made from a quiver tip passing through a table tennis ball. We had been using the dart float for a long time and catching lots of pike in the process. The only trouble with these floats was that, if there was a chop on the water and if the floats were any distance out, they were not really visible. With Vic and Eddie's float the large vane was the breakthrough to their success; the vane certainly caught the wind and it stood out like a lighthouse well over 100 yards away. The famous E.T. Drifter was born and I was to catch my first 30 on Abberton by using one of these. Although it was twenty-five years ago, it seems like yesterday, not least because that first 30 always stands out in your mind. I can well recall playing the pike in from over 100yd away, and I can still see that back and fin surfacing some 25yd out, just like a submarine. What an incredible high it gave me and I do really hope that the reader experiences that wonderful feeling at least once in his lifetime. Incidentally, I believe my fish was the first ever 30 caught on a drifter and although, as I mentioned, Abberton is a good doubles and even 20s water, 30s are quite rare. There have possibly only been a dozen or so caught in the last twenty years. One only wonders how many rod hours per fish that works out, especially as the reservoir is fished by at least three or four anglers every day throughout the season. Anyway, even with the present restrictions, I have some good days there with good friends, so let us hope that it continues.

What about the other reservoirs I have fished in the south east? The first thing to note is that, apart from Bewl Water in Kent, they have ceased to stock trout. The decline of trout fishing on such big reservoirs means that the chance of a really massive pike here has decreased. The waters will still produce some good pike in future, but probably no real monsters. It is a shame, but it seems that many of the trout reservoirs are going the same way. Even so, let us have a look at some of these reservoirs.

Ardleigh in Essex first opened for fishing in 1972. It is also near Colchester and comprises 120 acres, with a maximum capacity of 482

Steve Rodwell and Jason Davis breaking the ice at Ardleigh Reservoir.

million gallons of water. I first got to hear about it while fishing Abberton in the 1980s when an angler told me that pike were attacking trout as he played them in. I started to pester the Essex fisheries officer who used to visit Abberton, but he said that it was not worth piking on Ardleigh because it was netted on several occasions and the biggest pike caught was about 18lb. However, a year later, in 1987, I was amazed to read in the angling papers of a massive pike caught from there by Mike Linton. It weighed a mind-boggling 44lb 14oz, a new British record. So much for the unreliable information, but we decided that it would pointless immediately tearing down there since for the next few months every piker in the south east would be fishing it.

In fact, my first trip on Ardleigh was a year or two later with Steve Wells and Tony Corless. It proved to be very slow, but in the late afternoon Tony landed a nice 29lb specimen and I caught a 2lb perch on a small livebait. After seeing Tony's fish, I decided to spend a bit more time there and, three trips later, with a number of good doubles landed, I was to catch my first Ardleigh 20. I was boat fishing down the west arm in the bay and by the trout pens with a drifting bait towards the bank. I was running my baits on to the marginal shelf and, believe it or not, ended the day with not one 20 but a brace. During that first season Steve and I had several more 20s and, with the fishing getting better and better over the following few years, we had some fantastic days and catches, usually by trolling float-fished livebaits. When we were sharing a boat and the pike were on it was not unusual for us to have a dozen big doubles and a couple of 20s between us. One of my more memorable catches readily springs to mind.

My son Bernard, Steve Wells and I went out in two boats, with Steve being with me as he was fishing for only half a day and I had to get him back to the bank early. I started by trolling the main body of the reservoir, while Bernard made his way down the west arm. Just off the deep water, I had a screaming take, which resulted in a 22lb 8oz fish. Steve and I then had a couple of low doubles before we went back to the area where I had the 20. As we were over what turned out to be the hotspot, one of my baitrunners started to sing. Pulling into the fish, it stayed deep as it hugged the bottom. But the pressure eventually told and she broke the surface about 10yd from the boat. 'Blimey, it's a lump, Steve', I said, as my legs began to turn to jelly. By now she was on the top of the water as I slowly pulled her to the waiting net. As she came ever closer, I noticed that her gills were starting to flare. 'Please don't shake your head', I pleaded, as Steve finally slipped the net under her. The relief must have really been showing on my face as she went in, and we then left her in the net as we drifted back to the bank to do the weighing and the photographs. The weighing revealed that she was 31lb 8oz, at that time a new personal best. You can only imagine the exhilaration I felt as for the next couple of hours we concentrated our fishing on the hotspot. Another double was caught before Steve had to leave for work and so I dropped him off at the bank and headed up the west arm to see how Bernard had fared.

I had told Bernard to try the bay as I felt that there could be a good fish or two up there. On arriving there I saw that Bernard was anchored just off it and I dropped my baits back out, trolling my floats about 10yd behind the boat. 'How's it going, Bern?', I shouted across. 'Two big doubles and a big fish came off. Had any up the deep end, Dad?', was the reply. As I was about to answer, out of the corner of my eye I noticed that one of my floats was cutting fast across the water towards the bank. Quickly winding in the other rod, I struck into the fish. The rod slammed down and pulled the boat round, with the pike then circling the boat three times before I had her on top. Finally I managed to slip her into the net and it was another good fish. On reaching the bank, Bernard and I slipped her into the weigh sling with the needle pulling round to 28lb 8oz. Ten minutes later, would you believe, I was playing another big fish. I had it close to the boat a couple of times and it looked as big, if not bigger, than the 30 I had caught earlier. Suddenly, I felt a ping and I was sad to see a hook pulled out a couple of feet or so from the landing net. With another lunge she dived again and was gone.

Looking back at that day I could have finished up with a brace of 30s and 20s, but unfortunately it was not to be, but, having landed a personal best 30 and two 20s, I was not that disappointed (well, not too much). Indeed, that day was just one of the many great days Steve, Bernard and I had on Ardleigh during the 1990s. We, along with several friends, caught 30s, with my personal best going up a couple of times to 36lb 8oz in 1996. The reservoir kept fishing well up to the time that the water company ceased to stock trout. Today, Ardleigh is unlikely to produce monster pike, but as it has good stocks of perch and silver fish and it is still possible to catch good fish. For example, I had a day there in 2004 with a good friend Mem Hassan who was over from Thailand. After spending the morning catching perch and silver fish, we had a couple of hours' piking. We had five runs, resulting in two upper doubles and a low one. I believe that it is still worth a day's fishing and one or two 20s are beginning to come back out. Day tickets are available from the fishing lodge or the bank, and boats can also be obtained, but must be booked in advance.

Ardingly, near Haywards Heath, in West Sussex, is another large reservoir of 198 acres and produced very big pike when it was a trout fishery in the 1980s. Several 30s were coming out then and, although I did not fish it myself, mates such as Colin Benbrook and Roy Lyons did and with success. Colin caught a couple of 30s, with Roy being very unlucky since he has caught fifteen 20s here but not one went over 30, the biggest being 28lb 12oz. Roy's best day here was

Bill Palmer's boating partner Steve Wells with a reservoir big 20 caught on a float-trolled livebait.

in 1986 when he and Colin had travelled down after the hurricane the previous night. The causeway on the east bank was where he wanted to be, but fallen trees blocked the road and they had to park some distance away in the boathouse car park. Despite the long walk to the swim, it was more than justified with Roy's catching three 20s on paternostered lives – 28lb 12oz, 25lb 8oz and 20lb 8oz. Although now a coarse fishery only, to this day Ardingly still produces good-sized pike.

I first tackled Bough Beech Reservoir, near Tonbridge in Kent, in 1991. It is 226 acres in area and, during the early 1990s, because of the trout, it was throwing up a lot of big 20s, quite a few 30s and a massive fish of over 40lb, caught by Simon Marshall. Ken Crow ran the water and bent over backwards to help us to catch by supplying us with trout and even netting some silver fish for us to try. Although the trout are no longer around, Ken is and he told me there

could still be up to thirty different 20s, with one or two going over 30. Not least, he says, Andy Brown had a thirty-three pounder in December 2004, it being Andy's sixth 30 from the venue. Though it is a season-ticket water, there are bank and boat fishing, and bait may be caught or supplied by the fishery. Overall, it seems to be looking good for the future.

Darwell Reservoir, near Battle in East Sussex, has also declined as a pike water as the trout are no longer being stocked. Years ago it was run by the Hastings Fly Fishers Club and they used to allow us to pike fish a few days a year. We could livebait and trout were supplied by the club. Steve Wells's dad caught a 33lb monster from here, whereas my best was 28lb 12oz. Today the water is full of quality roach so, although monsters may be unlikely, you just never know what may turn up.

Finally, there is Bewl Water, which still is a picturesque trout reservoir near Lamberhurst in

Kent. It comprises 770 acres, with a depth of 80ft by the dam wall when full. I think that it was around 1979 when it was first opened for a limited amount of pike fishing. I was told that in the 1980s a number of pike of around 40lb were netted from the water. Steve Wells and I first tackled it in 1993 and I have tried to have a couple of days there every year since. I really do enjoy my days there despite the fishing restrictions, such as the use of only large sea deads and lures over 5in. I really do hate being restricted in my fishing and, with the late start and an early finish, it is probably what you would call a 'gentlemen's' day's pike fishing. Our best day was when we shared a catch of nine doubles with lots of small pike, with Steve taking the majority of them. However, if the trout continue to be stocked, I can see Bewl again turning up a real monster. One only has to recall Martin Godfrey's 41lb 12oz in January 2000, a repeat capture that Rob Dixon first caught at 41lb 8oz in December 1999. I shall certainly try to put some more time in there in the future since there are many features to search out and explore, and it is a very interesting and enjoyable reservoir to fish.

Incidentally, with the mention of features, it is opportune to stress the importance of these in relation to locating and catching reservoir pike, not just at Bewl, of course, but all reservoirs. There are obvious ones, such as overhanging trees and bushes and stream inlets and outflows, but others, such as drop-offs, which usually can be located only by, for example, plumbing the depths or talking to other pike anglers. All these features are potential pike-holding areas and need to be explored.

Lakes and Gravel Pits

Moving to lakes and gravel pits, there must be hundreds if not thousands of them across the south east. Few provide free fishing these days because angling clubs and syndicates run nearly all of them. They are often stocked with small carp for the pleasure or match angler, or large carp for the specialist. Nevertheless, many

contain a number of good-sized pike, and one or two are capable of giving up a real biggie from time to time. But where do you begin?

For a start, the more serious pike angler should consider the purchase of some Ordnance Survey maps of the area in which he is interested. You will soon be able to find some waters that may well hold pike. If you are prepared to walk a couple of miles or so with your gear over some rough ground or do a bit of climbing, there are still one or two out-of-the-way lakes or gravel pits that are not too heavily pike fished. Furthermore, the rewards can be really satisfying. Location is important and, especially in the case of gravel pits, it is often the bars and islands which provide the keys; for example, there may be parallel rows of islands running right across a pit, although every now and then there will be a break in this pattern, perhaps where a point sticks out or the pit narrows. This can leave a bay or a confluence of channels and that is as good as anywhere to start. By fishing two baits, one in open water and one close to an island where the island's shelf drops away quickly into deeper water, you have the chance of catching patrolling pike as well as those which have rested up.

During the 2004/05 season I have been doing a fair bit on an out-of-the-way gravel pit. Having to park the car a mile or so away, I have cut my gear down to the bare essentials. During the first five sessions I had been pre-baiting heavily in the chosen area. However, with no runs forthcoming I was getting rather worried that there might not be too many pike in the water. Consequently, I decided to put out two 'sleepers' to fish for me: two halves of mackerel, with a loop of cotton put through them, tied to some line and staked to the bank. Just as I was about to leave, one of the 'sleepers' was picked up and pulled free from the line. Removing the other 'sleeper' from the water, I cast two baits into the area where they had been. Within minutes one of my floats was running across the surface of the water before disappearing. Pulling into the fish, the rod bent and the pike was taking line. What a wonderful feeling that was; getting that first run and feeling the pike on a new and unknown water. The pike

ABOVE: A pre-baited 22lb 4oz gravel-pit pike for Bill Palmer.

Another gravel-pit pike for Bill Palmer, this time 24lb.

weighed 21lb and a couple of minutes later I was to have another of 20lb 8oz, then finishing with a 16lb. What a start, as all the baiting up was finally starting to work.

As I write, I am still putting in some time on this pit, fishing once or sometimes twice a week and baiting up when I leave. So how have my results gone? Well, I have fished twenty-one times, doing 4 to 6hr sessions at a time. Although I did not get a run until the fifth visit, I have now had thirty-two pike, thirty of which were doubles and fourteen over 20lb, to a best weight of 24lb. With only one small pike caught, I believe that, as soon as the bigger pike moved into the baited area, the jacks kept well away. On the last couple of sessions I also noticed that, often as I am pre-baiting at the end of the session, I have simultaneously had a run. Perhaps as the floats were being rocked by the bombardment of bait the pike regarded this as a dinner gong and moved to feed. I may have to start the bombardment at the start of my sessions.

As you can see, making the effort to find a pit or lake that is not pike fished regularly can lead to some tremendous fishing. Such waters may be few and far between, but they can still be found. For instance, did not Eddie Turner and Bill Hancock get an invitation from Keith Howard, the bailiff, to fish a chalk pit off the A13 in Essex many years ago? This pit was being back-filled and, as it became smaller, an area of sunken trees and bushes came into the reach of anglers. There is a long story to this water but, in short, it was to become an excellent pike venue. In particular, Eddie's fishing on the pit was to become unbelievable with his catching a number of 30s, including two braces, to 37lb 8oz. But it was not only Eddie who caught big pike. Tony Corless

Tony Corless with a 'Tescos' thirty-two pounder.

was also fishing there at the time, having been given a letter for permission to fish from Ray Pledger, and he used to take Steve Wells and Colin Benbrook as guests. They also caught decent pike, with Tony managing three 30s and Steve also getting one. Colin came close with a 28lb 8oz. It is worth pointing out that, when the back-filling started, the main body of the pit looked literally like milk with chalk and so for a time they fished Cotton Farm gravel pit, just across the river where Tony went on to have a number of 20s and a 30, as did Steve.

So what has become of the chalk pit, or 'Tescos' as it became known? After the back-filling to reach its present size, the reclaimed land was used to create the Lakeside Shopping Centre in Thurrock. Mike Toomer took over the

fishing lease for a while and stocked some big pike from Grafham Water. There were a number of 30s up to 38lb 8oz caught, and five months later I was to catch this last one at 26lb 2oz. She had lost almost 12lb in just five months and, although some of this was spawn, it was still a very big weight loss. Big trout-reservoir pike just do not seem travel well and are often soon lost. I believe that you can still fish at Tescos, but only in the deep pool at the A13 road end. The most productive area is now out of bounds as it is being used by scuba divers. It still is full of silver fish though, so with its pedigree more big pike are certainly on the cards.

There is no way in which I can write about gravel pits in the south east without mentioning the Warren. It was back in 1963 that I first fished

This thirty-eight pounder had lost 12lb when Bill Palmer caught her five months later at 26lb plus.

it with an old school mate Ray Alexander. We used to catch the train at East Ham, travelling to Stanford le Hope in Essex. Carp were the target then because we knew that there were no pike in the water at the time. In 1970 I used to do some eel fishing there, using small deadbaits, but again never picked up a pike. Then in 1983 Bernard caught our first pike from the Warren, a 7lb fish taken on a lobworm while tench fishing. On his next trip, fishing with half roach baits for eels, he was bitten off twice but eventually managed to land one of the culprits, a pike of 12lb. Some time later I was talking to another angler about Bernard's fish and the sudden appearance of such predators. The angler said that the bailiff reckoned he knew who was responsible, namely a bloke who drove a yellow

Ford Escort van with a pike painted on the side. Allegedly, he slipped pike into the water when no one else was around. 'Blimey, that's my van', I thought, although I can truthfully say, hand on heart, that it was not I.

In any case, by 1988 the pike were well established at the Warren and the following year Bernard and I were having a great time catching lots of big doubles from Hibsey's Corner and off the north bank. In 1991 Bernard had a fantastic couple of months, catching a number of 20s topped by two different 28s and a 30lb 8oz.

Then, in May 1993, the cat was let out of the bag when the Shell Angling Club netted the lake. Bernard's 30 turned up in one of the sweeps and bottomed out the 32lb scales, with the estimate being 35lb. Up until then I was keeping a very

Bill Palmer and a Warren 25lb 4oz.

low profile when piking here; I would set up my tackle so that I looked as if I was carp fishing, not using backbiters as indicators, for example. But news of the pike soon spread and in November 1993 a friend of Bernard, Barry Summerhayes, turned up at the Warren, having been thrown off his carp syndicate lake when it changed hands. He would have been carping that day and was not happy about losing his fishing, but, as one door shuts, fate provided another one for him to open. In short, on that day Barry went on to catch Bernard's fish at a whopping 39lb 8oz; she had put on another 9lb in two years.

The publicity from Barry's fish meant that the Warren got a lot more attention from pike anglers, including many of the 'names' beginning to show their faces. In December 1993 a 33lb, pot-bellied fish was caught, along with a 32lb caught twice on different days. Because of the extra angling pressure, some very good fish were appearing. John Smith had a cracking 32lb 8oz off the north bank and, as the 1993/94 season came to a close, a young lad caught a magnificent 34lb from Gorse Island. The Warren had certainly blossomed. Although the 39lb fish did not show, there was the capture of possibly three more different 30s. With a lot more anglers targeting the pike it was surprising that the big fish had not been caught again. I think that if she had still been alive she may have hidden herself away for winter, not having to move far as she picked off a 3–5lb jack as it swam by, or perhaps a big bream, tench or perch.

During the 1994/95 season I was unlucky not to catch a 30, landing a number of 20s, including the 33lb, pot-bellied fish at 25lb 4oz and one of the 30s twice at 27lb 4oz. But it was 17 July 1995 that turned out to be the fateful, never to be forgotten, day. I was fishing on a point near a concrete block; from here you can cover any patrolling pike as they hunt rudd shoals round the back island. On my first rod I put out a poly-balled rudd to the left, close to a large weed bed. On the other rod I lobbed another rudd the few yards to the reeds. The wind had picked up, funnelling through the point and blowing across on to Members Island. Suddenly, my right-hand

rod was away but the strike was into thin air as I missed. Recasting another bait to the same spot, I noticed that the left-hand rod's line was pouring from the spool. I wound down to the fish, but it felt as if I had pulled into a brick wall. The rod was bent right over as the pike then swam into the weed and everything went solid again. Suddenly, as I leaned into the pike, exerting as much pressure as I could, something gave and all that I wound in was a big ball of weed. Sadly, the fish had gone.

Bernard was making his way round to me and, as I told him what had happened, a big pike boiled exactly where I had lost the fish in the weed. I cast a rod there but the pike immediately came up again from where I had moved that rod. Seconds later, and right in front of us, the pike came up for a third time, but unfortunately it did not go back down as it struggled on the surface of the water. The wind was even stronger now and so it was difficult to see the fish properly, but, from what I could see, it looked very big, in particular, the dorsal fin and the tail, which waved as she toiled to get beneath the surface. 'Bern, that fish is in big trouble', I said, with him agreeing, 'Yeah, it don't look good, Dad.' The pike then drifted up against the reeds on the back island. I could have easily cast a set of hooks across its back and dragged the pike in, but you don't do that, do you? I even stopped Bernard from going around and pulling it out, telling him that the wind would move her before he got there. For another 15min the wind increasingly took its toll on the weakening pike as it drifted away, tail still waving at me, towards Members Island. Being sure that the dying pike was the one I had lost, I did not feel like continuing with the fishing and so I slowly packed up and went home. After working nights, the following morning I arrived home to find Sheila, my wife, sitting up and waiting for me. She immediately told me that Mick Toomer had telephoned after I had left for work the previous night saying that he had a 50lb dead pike. 'What?', I replied. 'A fifty pounder', she repeated. 'It's from the Warren, isn't it Sheila?' She wondered how I knew, but I did not answer as I quickly rang Mick. He had picked the pike up on the previous night after it had been found dying earlier in the day on Members Island. I said that I would be round straightaway and collected Steve Wells on the way, telling him what had happened. After arriving at Mick's and seeing the pike it simply took my, indeed our, breath away. She completely filled his jacuzzi; it really was a colossal fish, a monster fish and an absolutely mind-blowing sight. Steve and I could hardly believe what we saw.

We helped Mick to carry the pike to the garden for some photographs before she went on her final journey to the taxidermist. I had also remembered to slip a tape measure into my pocket as I left home since it was obviously important to have accurate measurements of such an historic fish. The total length was 51in, while to the fork of the tail she was 48½in and her girth was 29in. Mick later accurately weighed her on a brand-new set of Reuben Heaton 60lb scales and she registered 50lb 12oz. He told me that the pike was weighed on five different sets of scales with five different readings from 47 to 55lb. There was also talk of the pike perhaps taking in water and of a hose pipe being used, but I am not sure about all of this. What I can say is that, the amount of water it may have absorbed through its skin or taken in is anybody's guess, and a hose pipe was used only to keep it moist so that scales were not lost for the pictures. In addition, what I do know is that it had nothing in it when we weighed it and took the photos.

Anyway, after returning home and eventually going to bed, I was unable to sleep because of what had occurred. Three times I climbed into bed only to get up again as the events of the previous two days kept flooding back into my mind. Was it the good fish that I pulled out of in the weed? Why did I stop Bernard from going round to pull it out? Why did it die? For the next couple of days I was walking round like a zombie, not being able to work, sleep or eat. I could not even go to work and, on returning, my mates could not believe that I had taken time off over a fish. Indeed, it was months before I could get over the Warren monster, and I still think about

it to this day. If a relatively small water in Essex can produce such a 50lb pike, it may be your reservoir lake or pit that produces the next monster. I think there are certainly one or two waters in the south east that could be capable of doing so. They may not produce a 50lb pike, but certainly a 40lb specimen is a real possibility.

Methods, Rigs and Baits

Having looked at some of my favourite waters and memorable catches, I am often asked what are my preferred methods, what are the best rigs and baits and so on? To be honest, I believe that it does not really pay to have any favourites as you will probably find that you will end by using the same old method, rig or bait all the time. Echoing some earlier comments, you have to be versatile to be successful and my favourites tend to be the ones that I am using at the time to do the job. Mind you, having said that, there are some methods I enjoy more than others, as you would probably agree that it is not a lot of fun sitting behind a couple of deadbaits for hours on end just for one run. But I guess that if that is the method it takes to catch a big pike, so be it.

Anyway, my advice would be to first check out your chosen water by spending some time walking round with a rod, checking the depths and looking for such as weed beds, drop-offs, bars, bait fish and feeding grebes. If you are allowed to use a boat, by using a fish-finder the water can be soon be mapped out. The features I have just highlighted, like those mentioned earlier, are all potentially pike-holding areas.

As for actually starting fishing on a new water, if I were using three rods I would put out a ledgered popped-up deadbait on one, a paternostered livebait on the second and, if the wind were favourable, I would fish a livebait drifter on the third. Thus, with the first two rods fishing on alarms, I would be searching out as much water as I could by using the big vaned float on the third. If you are allowed to use a baitboat, then, even if the wind is not favourable for the drifter, you could still run it out in the baitboat. You could, for example, run it out for 100yd or more, then fish the drifter back across the water to you. An added bonus of using a baitboat is that your livebaits will not be damaged, as so often can happen when you are casting them. It goes without saying that it is great fun running out baits in a boat to distant features; after all, baitboats are great toys and surely we are all kids at heart.

It is worth saying that, if I were to be pushed into naming one of my most enjoyable methods of catching pike, as much of this chapter suggests, it would have to be float trolling from a boat. You get the feeling of total freedom, of being able to cover all the water, not least the features and the hotspots you could not reach from the bank. There is nothing better than catching baits for an hour or two, then, with your livebait bucket full, trolling over the expanse of a large reservoir, lake or gravel pit.

With regard to rigs and baits, the former I keep as simple as I can because there is no point in complicating them just for the sake of it. As for baits, my view is that lives will catch anything in the swim but deads are more likely to lead to the capture of bigger pike. I do not really have a favourite bait, rather I ring the changes as and when necessary until I find out what bait happens to be working at the time; it could be anything from sea deads such as mackerel, sardine or herring, to coarse deads such as roach, perch and bream. But remember, whatever method,

rig or bait you use, to make sure you that have excellent bite detection and that, when a bite occurs, do not hesitate but instead wind into the pike immediately and strike home.

There I guess you have it, a brief discussion of some of the waters I have pike fished in the south east of England over the last fifty years. There are dozens I have not mentioned and probably hundreds I have not fished, but I hope that the reader will have enjoyed and found useful some of my exploits and suggestions. I have enjoyed every minute of my pike fishing, not least being with good friends and catching some good pike along the way. Although I am lucky enough to live in an area that can produce some really good pike, it must be remembered that it was not always like this. In my early years I would be looking for waters that might produce a 20, but in the late 1950s such pike were very rare creatures. Most of the pike caught in those years were knocked on the head and taken home for the pot. Today many a pit and pond seems capable of producing 20lb pike. One factor to bear in mind is that the better handling and unhooking of pike mean that they go back alive which, in turn, leads to many more pike anglers getting a much better chance of a biggie or two. We have got to continue to look after our pike and our pike waters, so ensuring that there will be good fishing for many years to come. In the meantime, I would urge you all to get out there and experience at first-hand some of this wonderful sport of ours. Good luck to everyone.

9 PIKE FISHING IN WALES AND THE SOUTH WEST OF ENGLAND

Chris Donovan and Jon Cotton

Pike fishing in Wales and the south west of England might be more limited than in some other areas. For example, in central Wales game fishing predominates and pike are few and far between, while they are practically absent from Cornwall. This is one reason why we have lumped together Wales and the West Country in one chapter. Another is that pike anglers in the south west often fish in South Wales and vice versa. But, despite some of the foregoing, one should not run away with the idea that there is no good pike fishing to be had. Even though it may not be what it was, one has only to recall Llangorse Lake in South Wales, as well as Chew Valley Reservoir near Bristol, and Bala Lake and the River Dee in North Wales. The best of these waters though surely has to be Llandegfedd Reservoir, near Newport. Since the late 1980s it has produced numerous pike over the 35 and even 40lb mark, culminating in Roy Lewis's 46lb 13oz leviathan of October 1992. Furthermore, when one is pike fishing in such areas you may be in or near to some dramatic countryside and scenery, whether this is the mountains of Snowdonia or a mixture of the rolling hills and the verdant dales of other parts of Wales, and the south west of England itself also offers beautiful countryside as well as a spectacular coastline.

Not surprisingly, this chapter is divided into two. First, Chris deals with pike fishing in Wales, noting that, despite some earlier comments, South Wales in particular has been a hotbed of pike activity in recent decades, not just in terms of some memorable and exceptional catches but also of producing a group of anglers who have had an impact and influence on pike angling generally. Some of the main pike waters in Wales are also dealt with, along with the methods that have

led to success. Secondly, Jon looks at the pike fishing opportunities in the south west of England. There is good pike fishing to be had in areas such as Wiltshire and Dorset, not least because a sizeable length of the Hampshire Avon flows through these counties, and then there are the Dorset Stour and a large number of estate lakes and pits to consider. But here the focus is on the waters around Bristol, through Somerset to Devon, these providing some diverse pike fishing for the adventurous angler.

Wales

At the turn of the last century much of Wales must have been a desperate place for any budding pike angler who had aims of catching the king of freshwater fish close to home. As alluded to, the country in general had, and in some quarters still does, view itself as the home of game fishing and it has parallels with Scotland and Ireland in this regard. This attitude or ignorance has resulted in the persecution of pike as a species because of its perceived threat to game fish. In fact, the opposite is nearer the truth, with pike being the friend of the game angler by devouring the fish that compete with trout and salmon for food in both still-waters and rivers that run through this country of ours.

But generally, recent decades have been good for pike and the pike angler, especially in South Wales, with opportunities to catch pike becoming more readily available. For example, carp fisheries are even starting to catch on to the idea of the pike being a friend in the ecological predation game, with the more progressive clubs stocking and maintaining pike in their waters to reduce silver-fish levels for the benefit of carp growth rates. We can only hope that this attitude is contagious and that the future will be even kinder to pike and pike anglers.

My first experiences of pike came from a few small ponds in Newport, and it is extraordinary how such small ponds have been the starting point for many anglers, leading to our being

afflicted with the addiction we know as pike fishing. Even so, I am not egotistical enough to think that I have caught the pike that I have solely from my own efforts. It has been more the case of hard work, an attentive ear and a more general team effort, involving many participants. My circle of acquaintances has included Peter Climo, Bob Jones, Paul Sullivan, Phil Pearson and Will Travers. In their own ways, they have all helped and encouraged the improvement of Welsh piking either by making pike waters available to the general public or by showing what can be achieved if effort and knowledge are applied in the correct doses. One must not forget that, as anglers, we tend to learn from each other, although some would rather walk on hot coals than admit it. For instance, I learnt about pike location and where to fish from Paul and Phil, and they learnt from me where not to fish and so we tended to complement each other. Furthermore, Peter and Bob were the trail-blazers, not least in terms of their success in opening Llandegfedd to the public in the late 1980s, culminating with Peter catching a wonderful 42lb pike there. As for Paul and Phil, I started fishing with them in the late 1960s and they were the ones who eclipsed everyone else with their pike captures from this region and beyond. Pike fishing with all these, and others, has allowed me to piece together much relevant information until the jigsaw was complete, thus encompassing the journey from a little boy scratching around for a few small tench on the Monmouth Canal to battling alone for big pike on big waters and catching 30s into the bargain.

In looking at pike waters in Wales, let me begin with the south, although more accurately I mean the south

Peter Climo with his Mepps-spinner-caught 42lb 5oz from Llandegfedd.

Chris Donovan and his cracking Welsh best of 33lb 8oz.

east since this is where the main waters are. Geologically speaking, this area has been shaped by compression, which has led to the creation of a series of mountainous valleys that spread from Swansea in the west to Newport in the east. This mountainous scenery is ideal for the construction of reservoirs that provide much of the water available to the pike angler. Natural pike waters of any significance were few and far between before the construction of the reservoir system and amounted to sections of the rivers Severn and Wye, Llangorse Lake, Kenfig Pool and a small number of waters averaging under 50 acres in size. Indeed, the Severn and the Wye can be seen as Wales' gift to England since they rise in the Welsh mountains before entering England and eventually discharging into the Severn estuary. Interestingly, this path offers an anomaly whereby if you caught a 30lb pike from the Severn in Wales it would, of course, be a Welsh 30, but the same sized fish in Worcester would be an English 30, although it came from the same river. Even stranger is the fact that, if you caught a 30 from the mouth of the River Monnow at Monmouth you would be a proud captor of a Welsh 30, but if you were lucky

enough to catch the same fish across the other side of the river it would be an English 30. It would not worry me either way, but it is a fact for the statistically minded. Be that as it may, my pike fishing actually began on a natural still-water.

Llangorse Lake was the venue that opened my eyes to the wonders of pike fishing. It all began in the early1970s when a small group of keen pike anglers started to fish this large lake situated in the Brecon Beacons, created by the River Llynfi on its path to the Wye. Reputed to be a migratory path for salmon, it used to hold numbers of large pike, with one only having to recall the fish of 68lb caught by Owen Owen in 1846. Even so, it was not considered to be a regular 30 water, despite its remote location and the absence of pike-angling pressure in the early days. But this changed when large shoals of big bream started to show in numbers, when previously only perch, eels and roach had been the main prey for pike; as we know, big bream mean big pike and Llangorse was no exception.

As with all waters, successful piking meant that you had to move around the lake, anchoring at as many as half a dozen swims or more in a day's fishing, and by doing this Paul and Phil had the bulk of the big fish in those early days. It is for them to tell the angling fraternity of their successes, but I can say that the methods they honed to perfection on Llangorse went on to lead to success on other waters such as Irish loughs and Scottish lochs. Later, float-trolled live and dead-baits, and more recently the inclusion of float-trolled silicones by myself, added to the armoury, leading to the capture of many big pike over the years. The in-line paternoster rig was perfected at Llangorse and this allows your bait to remain static in even the worst conditions of wind and drag. The in-line surface rig was another innovation, particularly for shallow water, but was also effective when fishing just below the surface in deeper water with livebaits. Fifteen doubles in a day to one angler is the best haul that I heard of from those days and multiple 20 catches were not a rare occurrence. I remember one

great day when two others and I shared in a haul that included two 20s.

Unfortunately, Llangorse is now a shadow of its former self and shows no sign of recovering its glory, but current anglers who are not aware of its past potential may disagree and be satisfied with their results. But anglers in the know are fully aware of the demise of the water largely due to netting, the killing of pike by the unenlightened, cormorant predation on the food supply and overfishing by pike anglers. There are now a disproportionate number of jacks, which is a sure sign of a dysfunctional and unbalanced fishery, although, of course, there are still some bigger pike to be had.

Turning now to the Severn and the Wye, they rise close to each other in mid Wales and both have large stocks of pike. Thirty-pound pike are caught every year and my best river pike of 28lb 8oz was recently caught there, so that there are

Bob Jones with a 23lb 14oz beauty from the River Wye.

certainly specimens to be had. It has been only in the past four years that I have concentrated on them for my winter sport and had a fair amount of success into the bargain. As with one's experience with all waters, there is a learning curve and I cannot disclose precise fishing locations on these rivers because they were given to me by friends, but the well-known sections of the Severn are at Montgomery, Abermule and Newtown all in Powys. As for the Wye, Monmouth town centre, where there is a wide (some 90yd) and initially slow stretch, is well known, as is the river at Bigsweir off the A466, Monmouth– Chepstow road. All these areas can produce pike. As with all river pike fishing, location is the key and examples of likely pike-holding areas are the deep waters on oxbow bends, on the edges of reeds and weeds, alongside overhanging trees and bushes and near bridges. The reader will be only too well aware of the importance of such features when it comes to river pike fishing. It is also important to fish these rivers when they are at their prime, which is just after a flood when the water starts to clear and the levels are dropping. My advice is to bide your time and fish when conditions are in your favour rather then battle away for hours when the chances of catching are virtually zero.

I may also add that my results dramatically increased when I started fishing the more popular stretches of these rivers and had moved away from the more remote sections. Most of the Wye in particular falls into the 'remote' category and the private game fisheries that predominate here do not always produce as might have been expected. Admittedly, there are some parts that buck this trend, so in reality any part of the river is able to produce big pike. However, the stretches of the river where matches are held are the ones I favour. Masses of dace and chub are attracted because of the weekly deluge of breadcrumbs and maggots thrown in by the match anglers. It is no surprise that such anglers are plagued by pike striking in their swims, and not far behind will be the pike angler. Indeed, it is not hard to see that a good tip is to attract dace and chub to your swim, much as match anglers do, and the pike will soon appear. Similar

comments apply equally to the Severn, although my experience there is limited to one very up and down season. It could fish brilliantly and hopelessly in equal measures depending on the weather, which, in turn, affects the water flow, clarity and temperature.

I now want to make some comments on reservoir pike fishing in Wales, particularly in South Wales. At the outset it should be noted that during the early part of the last century Britain engineered an expansion of water capacity that resulted in the building of a large number of reservoirs, and South Wales was no exception. From the five Heads of the Valley reservoirs above Merthyr Tydfil that run northerly from Pontsticill to Talybont, to the magnificent Llandegfedd Reservoir just outside Newport in the south there are reservoirs of varying shape and size and most hold pike, although not all are accessible to the pike angler. Nevertheless, they all have the potential to produce specimen-size fish.

These reservoirs were originally designated as trout-only waters by the powers that be, but they also provide an ideal environment for pike as well as other coarse fish. At first I was not totally convinced that pike flourished there because of the trout, since in the early Llandegfedd days some of the removed pike were found to have only coarse fish in their stomachs. However, if comparisons are made between two very similar reservoirs, such as Llandegfedd and Pontsticill, it becomes quite clear that the trout do make a difference since the results from these waters are so different, with the former being prolific in terms of large pike and the latter, not now being stocked with trout, less so.

The jewel in the crown of pike fishing in Wales has to be Llandegfedd in my view. It has only a few spawning areas and these, together with plummeting waters levels in early spring, can have a profound effect on the successful spawning and fishing of all species. The early successes here can be put down to the higher water levels in the spring during the 1980s, and the anglers who managed to fish there then certainly reaped the rewards. Phil Pearson, in particular, caught many big pike during these early days and then, as now, moving baits such as sink and draw deadbaits and lures seemed to out-fish everything else. Livebaiting would, of course, have been a killer method if permitted, but static deadbaits were less effective. In recent years Llandegfedd has struggled a little to maintain its place at the head of the big-pike waters, but it can still throw up a surprise as shown by a big 30 which was was caught during summer 2003 during a lure-only event.

Ponsticill is a different matter in that the last 30lb pike that I am aware of was caught in the early 1980s when trout were still being stocked. The absence of any deep-water species may also be a factor since the reservoir is very deep, up to 100ft, with fish shoals regularly found only at 40ft. With hindsight, I have wasted many a day fishing in the bottom 80 to 100ft of water when the pike are generally caught in 20 to 30ft, with static deadbaiting being the preferred method.

As indicated, you might as well forget pike fishing when it comes to central Wales. It is fairly inaccessible and mountainous with few coarse fishing waters, let alone potential pike waters. However, in the north there are several pike waters of note. They may not all compare well with some of the waters to the south but they can by productive both in terms of the numbers and size of fish. For example, Richard Mark, the former regional organizer of the North Wales area of the Pike Anglers Club, is said to have witnessed a fish of 41lb from Bala Lake. He has also referred to the examination of a carcass of a Bala pike by Liverpool University, which was estimated to be some 46lb. Admittedly, all this was some years ago, and it goes without saying

The traps are set on Bala Lake.

that such fish are very rare indeed. A far more realistic target for anyone visiting the area would be a double-figure or a 20lb fish.

When it comes to North Wales pike waters more generally, two that contain pike are Llyn Bran and Llyn Aled on the Denbigh Moors. The latter is some 110 acres in area and has some decent coarse fishing, including some big perch and, not least, some decent pike. There is also the Llangollen Canal to note, but surely the most famous waters of the area are Bala Lake and the River Dee.

Bala Lake, or Llyn Tegid as it is also known, is the largest natural lake in Wales, being 4 miles long and ¾ mile wide. It is set in the mountains of Snowdonia and contains trout, roach, perch and eels, as well as the rare gwyniad, a land-locked whitefish, so it is not really surprising that some big pike can also be had. It can be hard going, though, and it is probably best not to expect to catch on your first visit but rather to use this trip to explore and get your bearings. I would advise the use of a boat, but bank fishing can also be productive, but if you are doing this at the town end remember not to fish more than 30yd out as it can be very deep and barren. Lures and sea deadbaits work equally well, particularly when trolled. Access is on either side of the lake via the lay-bys and car parks on the A494 or the B4403.

The River Dee is often thought of a game fishery and rightly so, but downstream from Llangollen to Chester it also produces coarse fish, including some large pike. It may not be as productive as it once was but it is still well worth a visit. For instance, Bangor-on-Dee (Bangor-is-y-coed) provides a pleasant stretch of the river with lots of chub, grayling, dace and eels and so it is not surprising that pike are also to be caught. Similar comments apply to the river at Overton and Cefn Mawr. As with all rivers, generally it is best to fish the Dee in its slower, deeper stretches that have features such as oxbows and overhanging trees and bushes. Concentrate on these areas with the usual methods using dead and livebaits, as well as lures, and it will not be long before pike are caught.

The South West of England

Moving to the south west of England, the importance of consulting the relevant Ordnance Survey maps cannot be overestimated, but let us begin with a look at the Bristol Avon. It rises close to the town of Malmesbury before meandering through some stunning scenery around Chippenham, Bath, Keynsham and Bristol, before entering the Severn Estuary at Avonmouth, just west of Bristol. Like most rivers, its character can change with the turn of each bend, ranging from fast, shallow stretches inhabited by barbel and chub to slower, deeper reaches with a good head of bream and roach. Add to these healthy stocks of dace, eels and perch, with carp and tench in some areas, and it is clear to see that the pike population is well fed.

The Avon has produced pike over 30lb in the past and is relatively under-fished in many areas, so, for the angler prepared to travel light and cover a great area of water in the course of a day's fishing, there are rewards to be reaped. A realistic target for the visiting angler would be a mid-double fish, but the chance of a really big fish cannot be ruled out. I cannot boast an Avon 20 but maybe I have not given the river the attention it deserves. I can say that all recognized pike fishing methods work well, with lure fishing being a good way of tackling a lot of water, and perhaps using deadbaits when a concentration of pike has been located. Access points are legion, especially in the city centre stretches of Bath and Bristol, and between the cities too, since for places such as Limpley Stoke, Saltford and Swineford access can be obtained from the A4. Upstream of Bath the A36 runs parellel to the river and gives good access around Claverton and Avoncliffe. A word of warning, though: the river suffers from some spectacular winter floods, being virtually unfishable for days on end. So consult the Environment Agency if you are in any doubt about the condition of the river.

Moving 10 miles south of Bristol and nestling in the Mendip Hills, we come to the Chew Valley Reservoir, which was created by damming the Chew in the early 1950s. It is some 1,200 acres

A 16lb fish for Jon Cotton in the early days. It came from the Bristol Avon.

in extent when full, but it is by no means a huge, featureless sheet of water. Rather it is a relatively shallow lake with a maximum depth of 37ft at the dam end, but averaging around 14ft. It has a large area of shallows and it is these that provide an abundance of aquatic life, along with an ideal spawning habitat for Chew's enormous head of coarse fish, namely roach, perch and pike. Chew became one of the first artificial trout fisheries in the United Kingdom in 1956 and soon became established as one of the top trout waters in the country. In the late 1980s it was apparent that there was a healthy pike population and it was not long before local PAC members were making approaches to Bristol Water with a view to gaining access. Throughout the 1990s such request fell on deaf ears, with the company maintaining that the pike had been illegally introduced by the very anglers who now wanted to fish for them. Each spring saw numbers of pike removed and transferred to other waters such as the Cheddar Reservoir 15 miles to the south.

By the early 2000s, however, Bristol Water recognized the source of income that pike anglers represented and opened up Chew to them, first for pike fly-fishing and then to a series of organized pike-fishing events, allowing lures and sea deadbaits. These events are fished in February and October–November every year and have proved very successful. It soon became clear that this was a pike water of exceptional quality, with every year since seeing Chew 30s adorning the pages of the angling weeklies, culminating in a new venue record of 38lb 8oz by Darren White in early 2005.

As with any large water, a boat represents the best option to get the most of out of Chew, but it is interesting to note that Darren's fish was taken from the bank in less than 3ft of water. The water also responds well to sea deadbaits, with most types scoring. My own personal best of 25lb 8oz was taken on a paternostered smelt in 2ft of water in Heron's Green Bay in 2001. But drifting is a good tactic, sometimes with a drogue to slow the drift. Casting lures in front of the boat and trolling a couple of deads behind also works well. You can locate groups of feeding pike and then anchor up and make the most of the situation. Areas such as Roman Shallows, Hollow Brook, Stratford Bay, as well as Heron's Green Bay, are all worth exploring in this way. And later in the year the area in front of Woodford Lodge becomes thick with fry and it is here that many of the bigger fish can be found in the autumn,

ABOVE: Jon Cotton and a nineteen pounder from Stratford Bay, Chew Valley Reservoir.

BELOW: A personal best of 25lb 8oz for Jon Cotton from Heron's Green Bay, Chew Valley Reservoir.

along with some sizeable perch, particularly around the landing stages.

Crossing into Somerset, we come to the Cheddar Reservoir, which is tucked away at the foot of the Mendip Hills on the edge of the Somerset Levels. It is about 400 acres when full and is a water supply reservoir of the 'concrete bowl' variety, having two parts in terms of access and depth. First, the Axbridge side is relatively shallow for the most part with depths rarely exceeding 12ft and it can be very weedy. Access is through the village of Axbridge and is well signposted from the A371; a rod pod is essential here since the banks are solid concrete. Secondly, continuing along the A371, we reach the Cheddar side, which is deeper, up to 25ft within casting distance, and favoured by pikers in winter; in particular, swims close to the 'Vee', the water inlet, receive a lot of attention.

Deadbaits work well at Cheddar, with ledgered and paternostered presentations taking most of the fish. However, it is also worth having a drifter set-up handy for those days when the pike are well offshore, and at Cheddar it can be a long way indeed. In recent years fish of 25lb have been produced and 20s are landed every season, although a realistic aim would be a couple of mid double-figure pike. Personally, it was always my bogey water as I always seemed to be a day early or a day late, or walk past swims that produce for anglers who simply turn up and sling out any old bait.

We now come to the Somerset Levels, an area of about 200sq. miles situated between the Bristol Channel to the west, the Mendip Hills to the north, Glastonbury to the east and the Quantock and Blackdown Hills to the south. It is a haven of peace and isolation for anglers, walkers, birdwatchers and wildfowlers. Most of it is below sea level and is drained by a veritable maze of rivers, drains, ditches and rhynes which

This nice 22lb 2oz fish was caught by Jon Cotton on the River Brue.

provide a wide variety of fishing and, in particular, some excellent pike fishing. The levels are neatly divided in half by the Polden Hills, with the River Brue and its associated drains lying to the north and the River Parrett system to the south.

The waters of the Brue have been providing quality pike fishing for donkey's years and the sheer volume of water means there is something for everyone. The river itself is shallow, relatively fast flowing and canalized in its upper reaches from above Glastonbury down to Westhay. Here there is a good head of chub, roach, dace and bream. From Westhay down to its confluence with the Severn Estuary at Highbridge, it becomes deeper and steadier with bream, tench and carp being dominant. Throughout the river, however, pike are to be found with some excellent sport to be had, especially by the angler prepared to cover a lot of water in a day. I have taken seven 20s in recent years, including a cracker of 24lb 4oz in the winter of 2004, all between Westhay and Highbridge. These Brue pike are incredibly fit fish, largely a result of their battling the very strong flows that occur in times of flood, an all too regular experience in our increasingly wet winters. Indeed, the pike fishing tends to be at its finest just before and immediately after a flood, and some of my best days have been when it is wet. It might not be very comfortable for the angler but, in my experience, the pike love it. Bright sunshine, on the other hand, seems to be the kiss of death.

A leapfrogging approach is a good way to start out, maybe moving every 20min or so until fish are located, then spending longer exploring an area once fish have ben found. The pike here are very mobile, so an area full of pike one week may be deserted the next. More recently I have found lure fishing to be an effective way to search out pike. Once I had fished nearly a mile of water with nothing to show for my efforts; stopping at a small farm bridge for a much needed drink, I cast a Shad Rap upstream and half-heartedly began the retrieve. Imagine my surprise when *three* pike followed the lure right to the bank. Out went two deadbait rods and, coupled with

lures, I took twelve fish including a 20, a high double and two good mid-doubles in 3hr from a 50yd stretch of water. Next week – you have guessed it, nothing. So I guess that it is back to the hunting approach again.

Mention should be made of the South and the North Drain, which are typical land drains, averaging 3ft in depth and about 25yd wide, although the former widens to 50yd below Chilton Polden down to its junction with Huntspill and Cripps at the Gold Corner Pumping Station. Both waters have produced pike to well over 25lb in the past but have been somewhat in the doldrums of late. This could be because of increased cormorant activity, the reintroduction of otters to the Brue valley or just part of the natural cycle. There are still plenty of pike to be had, but to locate them has proved increasingly tricky. Since both waters are mostly dead straight, any feature, however small, can produce. For example, members of the local PAC were holding a junior teach-in at Shapwick on the South Drain. I was paired with a young lad who had never pike fished before. I suggested that he put a bait near a small weed bed directly in front on the near bank. All his mates were casting to the far bank and so he did likewise – everyone knows that pike live far away, don't they? I let him carry on and quietly dropped one of my baits alongside the weed. Within 5min the herring was taken and, after a short tussle, a corker of 18lb 14oz was banked. My young companion was gobsmacked but he had learnt a valuable lesson the hard way.

The Huntspill Drain is easily the biggest water on the Levels, being 8 miles long and well over 100yd wide in places. It is completely man-made, originally to supply water to the nearby Ordnance Factory at Puriton, but it also proved to be an effective way of draining the land of the Brue valley by providing another outflow to the Bristol Channel. It is renowned for its bream, but, although all the waters connected to it contain quality pike, the Huntspill is something of an enigma since it has no great track record in terms of big pike, nor of pike in any quantity. In fairness, it probably does not receive much attention from local pikers, apart from the Gold Corner area,

The South Drain at Shapwick, Somerset.

which gets packed with roach and bream in winter. For years the Huntspill was regarded as a barren, featureless expanse, but recent landscaping carried out by the Environment Agency and English Nature has seen treacherous, steep banks being improved, reed beds planted and fry refuges created in an attempt to prevent fish from being swept out to sea during times of heavy winter run-off. As a result, perhaps it will become home to a more balanced fish population and, as more pikers turn their attention to this under-fished water, there could be a big surprise or two lurking in its depths.

Finally, in relation to the Brue, there is the Cripps River, which is a small watercourse of 2 miles that connects the Brue above Bason Bridge to the Huntspill and the South Drain at Gold Corner. During winter floods roach and bream from the Brue 'sit' here out of the strong flows and the pike often follow. Fully authenticated pike to over 30lb have been produced from here although, more realistically, fish to 20lb can be expected.

Let us now turn our attention to the Parrett system, with the main watercourses of interest to the pike angler being the River Parrett itself, along with the rivers Tone, Yeo and Isle, the Kings Sedgemoor Drain, the West Sedgemoor Drain, the Sowey River and the Bridgwater to Taunton Canal. Here I shall deal with the waters with which I am most acquainted.

The River Parrett is heavily tidal from Oath Lock down to Bridgwater, and coarse fishing, and hence pike fishing, is best around the town of Langport. Here the river is wide, deep (up to 10ft plus) and steady flowing. Fish to mid-20s are taken from here every year. Above the pumping station at Huish Episcopi is also a highly rated area, particularly where the Yeo joins. The river here is narrower, with more bends and features to aim at, whereas the lower reaches are more canalized and more of a barren, featureless nature. The area around Combe, where the sluice that forms the start of the Sowey River is situated, is popular with pike anglers and produces good numbers of pike to deadbaits and lures. Overall, the Parrett is a sizeable piece of water much of which remains unexplored in terms of piking potential. I for one would have spent a lot more time there if I could have torn myself from the Kings Sedgemoor Drain and the Sowey River.

The Kings Sedgemoor Drain is one of the oldest man-made waters on the Levels, having been created in the late eighteenth century to increase the agricultural land as well as to raise money for the Crown estate. It is some 7 miles in length and for the angler the most popular stretches extend from just above Greylake sluice on the A361, Taunton–Glastonbury road, down to Dunball clyce (a sluice gate), where the drain is crossed by the A38. Access may be gained at both of these points, along with good access from the A39 just outside Bridgwater and from the villages of Bradney, Chedzoy and Weston-zoyland, all easily reached from the A39. The drain itself is relatively narrow, about 30yd, from Greylake down to where the Sowey merges, widening to 40–50yd below the Sowey mouth. The depth is a constant 7–8ft from Greylake to Bradney, where it increases to 10ft with deeper spots in places. It is home to a good

Jon Cotton and a fine 21lb 4oz fish from the Kings Sedgemoor Drain.

head of pike of all sizes, which respond to sea deadbaits and lures in particular, and I have found that baits such as sardine, smelt or herring presented on float ledger or paternoster tackle tend to produce. The pike are quite spread out early in the season and, although the access points I have mentioned produce numbers of pike, they are heavily fished. Once again, the roving angler can expect better sport than the guy who slings out two deadbaits right by the car park and proceeds to sit there all day. I rarely fish the access points, preferring to walk half a mile or so before starting to fish. This approach has reaped dividends in recent seasons, with fish to 22lb falling to me on a fairly regular basis. I spend no more than half an hour in one spot, unless there is evidence that pike are present, before moving along the drain in search of that elusive monster.

As for the Sowey, the name is misleading as its full title is the Parrett Flood Relief Channel, another man-made drain rather than a full-blown river. It runs from the River Parrett at Combe to the south east and joins the Kings Sedgemoor Drain below Greylake, a distance of abut 6 miles. It is like the drain but a lot narrower, and access is from the A361 below Greylake sluice or from the A372 between Othery and Langport. The fishing here is free although a rod licence is required.

The Bridgwater–Taunton Canal was built in the nineteenth century and passes through a number of villages en route. Access is easy with car parks being signposted from the A38 and the A361. The canal itself is shallow, with depths rarely exceeding 4ft and it is fairly narrow, about 30ft, although it widens at times and especially towards Bridgwater. There are lots of jacks although doubles are to be had, especially with lures in the warmer months. The canal also has the advantage of being fishable when all the other waters in the area are flooded, since the

coloured water from the Tone does not seem to dent the pike's feeding habits. In times of coloured water, sea deads work well.

Leaving the Levels, we come to the River Exe and the Exeter Canal. The former is an excellent game river but it and its associated canal contain a good head of coarse fish, including some very large pike. The canal in particular produces 20s every year although it can be a tough nut to crack. It is especially deep for a canal, being 15ft or more in places, and it can be up to 100yd wide especially around the Lime Kilns area. The water is usually clear, with the pike responding to all methods fished close to features. Access is via car parks in the town-centre, at the swing bridge where the A379 to Dawlish crosses the canal or at Lime Kilns and Turf Lock, off the A379 just outside Exeter.

The River Exe is limited in terms of accessible stretches, as many are strictly for salmon anglers, but the tidal river from Countess Weir downstream along with the town-centre sections are open to pike anglers. It is relatively lightly pike fished, but the fact that there are lots of bream and roach, along with mullet and bass, coupled with runs of salmon and sea trout, suggest that there ought to be some fine piking to be had.

In concluding, we hope that we have provided a taster of the pike fishing opportunities in Wales and the English south west. As well as looking at some of the main waters, we hope that the reader will have found some helpful advice, tips and guidance. Clearly there are other pike waters in this area of the country but it would take a whole book to cover them all. If this chapter has succeeded in giving some insights into the types and styles of pike angling in our areas then it will have been worthwhile. If you should decide to pay us a visit, we wish you tight lines, tight braids and good pike fishing.

10 PIKE FISHING IN SCOTLAND

Steve Ormrod

Scotland ... the very word conjures up some vivid images, even to the angler who has never been there. Big skies and lands reflected in wild waters is a good description of the country, and when it comes to the pike fishing these waters really are in a class of their own. Scotland can be a pike angler's paradise, not least because there are waters of every kind. They range from big, wind-swept lochs at the base of huge mountains, to beautiful lochans nestled in pine forests. There are wild, clear rivers, which begin as charging streams before roaming through picturesque glens. And then there are the often neglected, at least in terms of pike fishing, canals. This is just a taste of what awaits the avid angler because the majority of these waters are home to rod-bending pike that are likely to have never been caught before. Scottish pike really are some of the hardest fighting fish you will ever encounter, being typically long, quite lean and superbly marked with uniquely pointed tails. Even small fish will give you a scrap and test your gear and skill to the limit. There is something here for all branches of our sport. Whether you prefer to boat fish and search the pike out with lures or to set up camp and static bait fish a chosen feature, Scotland has it all.

But there is much more to Scotland than just the fabulous pike fishing and scenery. It is a country rich in wildlife, especially in the more remote areas. Sightings of ptarmigan, osprey and even a golden eagle are a possibility, along with other birds. Many animals can also be seen, including red deer (especially in the noisy rutting season), otters, seals, adders, badgers, mountain hares, pine martens, red squirrels and the elusive wildcat. For such a small country, Scotland really does have a diverse range of animals, many of which cannot be found elsewhere

in Britain. Add to this the renowned hospitality and friendliness of the Scottish people and you cannot ask for anything else.

In this chapter I begin with a look at some of the main pike waters and in so doing divide the country into southern Scotland, central Scotland and the Highlands. These divisions relate to lochs but there are also rivers and canals to consider, so I then briefly deal with them. Also included in this section are some notable catches and piking stories. Finally, I look at favourite tactics, rigs and baits when tackling Scotland's pike waters.

It may be stating the obvious, but the waters I refer to below constitute by no means a comprehensive list. Many others contain pike and need to be fully explored. Much of eastern Scotland, for instance, is relatively unfished for pike. Furthermore, there are some good waters to be found on the Western Isles, with the Isle of Bute and lochs Fad and Ascog being of note. But perhaps I digress a little, so let us look at some of the main pike waters in the areas mentioned.

Southern Scotland

The main pike fishing area in southern Scotland is in the west. Heading north as you leave England just past Carlisle, if you go towards Stranraer on the A75 you enter Dumfries and Galloway. It is an area rich in pike waters, including the famous Loch Ken along with the almost equally well known Castle Loch at Lochmaben. There are numerous others such Auchenreoch, Milton and Woodhall lochs, while further west you will find the likes of Clatteringshaws, Ronald, Heron and Maberry lochs. But there are many others which, although relatively small, are also well worth exploring.

It is Loch Ken though that is the jewel in the crown of this area as it is steeped in legend, with the Kenmure pike of 1774, which reputedly weighed an incredible 72lb. The loch is basically a giant, shallow river basin, being 10 miles long, with the River Dee flowing into and out of it. A lot of pike are present, although you may have to get through the jacks to catch a larger fish. Even so, there is a good chance of fish to about the mid-20s mark. The best way to tackle it is from a boat since there are so many small bays to cover, although bank fishing is also productive. Access is available along the whole length of the eastern shoreline, from the A713 from Castle Douglas. On the west, easy access is from the south of New Galloway on the A762. It fishes well in the winter and is also an excellent roach venue. Perch and bream are abundant too, making it rich in natural prey. Some recognized areas of interest include the 'birches and boulders' stretch on the New Galloway side and Glenlaggan on the eastern side. Signal crayfish can be a pest on Ken, stripping your baits in a matter of minutes; this is avoided by popping up your baits off the bottom or paternostering them.

Mention has been made about one's having to get through the jacks to get to the larger fish, but this is well worth the effort as Paul Grimsley knows only too well. He has pike fished in south-west Scotland since he was a teenager. When he was made redundant, his uncle moved to Lochmaben because of the pike fishing and Paul and his friends used to go up as often as they could. They have fished all of the lochs referred to here, but Ken has always been the one where they have had most success. This was especially so in March 1998. Paul and his friends were on Ken yet again and had caught lots of pike to double figures. One of the jacks, of about 1lb, was deeply hooked and it was doubtful whether it would survive and so Paul decided to use it as a ledgered deadbait. It was gently cast out into a small bay, after which he and his friends continued to have pike action although no really big fish were being caught. But suddenly he noticed that line was peeling off the reel of the rod with the jack on. The adrenalin started pumping as the bail arm was set and he struck home. At first the rod bent solid and he thought that he had hit a snag, but then the slow movement of a powerful fish told him that a big pike had snaffled the jack. It was several minutes before the fish came to the surface and started shaking its head and jaws and thrashing its tail. Paul immediately knew it was the biggest pike he had ever seen, let alone caught. Gradually he brought her to the bank for the netting, with the thought 'it's got to be a 30' running through his mind. His friends readily agreed as she was quickly unhooked and weighed with the

Paul Grimsley and his mammoth 37lb 2oz from Loch Ken.

scales revealing a magnificent 37lb 2oz. Photos, of course, were hastily taken before the splendid specimen was carefully returned to the water where she eventually slowly swam back into the depths of the loch.

Moving to Ayrshire, north of Dumfries and Galloway but before you reach Glasgow, there is Loch Doon off the A713. This is a big water, with a good head of trout and a decent salmon run too. It is part of the hydroelectric power system linked by river to Clatteringshaws Loch. I have no information on the pike potential, but it again could well be worth a look, especially as the fishing is free. There are also lochs Kilbirnie and Castle Semple at Lochwinnoch which are renowned coarse fisheries.

Central Scotland

We now come to central Scotland, which is dominated by the most famous of Scottish pike waters, namely Loch Lomond. Then, in the Queen Elizabeth Forest Park to the east of Lomond, lie lochs Katrine, Venacher, Achray, Lubnaig, Ard, Chon and Arklet and so there is certainly a lot of choice. Nestled among them is 'the lake of dreams', the Lake of Menteith, which is, in fact, Scotland's only lake (as opposed to lochs, of course). It regularly produces 30lb pike, although only privileged yearly access to the Pike Anglers Club and the Pike Anglers Alliance of Scotland is allowed. Finally, in the north west of the region there is the great Loch Awe, and surely its name says it all. All of these lochs can produce some excellent pike fishing but it is Lomond, Awe and Menteith that warrant further comment.

Loch Lomond is 22 miles long and up to 5 miles wide, thereby having the largest surface area of any freshwater mass in the United Kingdom. Its pike reputation needs no introduction and it remains a Mecca for many pike anglers today. It has a good mix of both game and coarse species, including vast shoals of large roach. The best sport can usually be found in its southern half, this being much shallower than the northern

deeps. The loch is at its widest in the south too and has many feature islands.

Even if you are struggling to catch, just being on Loch Lomond surrounded by beautiful countryside and mountains makes it all worthwhile. But although it is a big water, bank fishing is restricted because much of the surrounding land is in private hands so the best way to tackle it is afloat. Some of the better areas are near the river mouths, the most famous being the Endrick bank in the south east, where a well known, productive drop-off lies about 70yd offshore. One of Lomond's great legendary discoveries was the Endrick pike in 1934, reputedly weighing a staggering 70lb. Balmaha & McFarlane's boatyard are not far away, making boat hire easy to fish this area. There is also some bank fishing off the shore and off the pier where some deep water can be found. The roach shoals gather here in the winter months and so do the pike. Drumkinnon Bay near Balloch is another good roach-holding area since they tend to go up the nearby River Leven to spawn.

Lomond's north holds Ardlui Bay, which comes a close second in popularity with pike anglers. Here the roach tend to be replaced by large perch shoals, which the pike readily feed on. Finally, over on the west bank is the neglected area around the village of Luss, which can be surprisingly productive.

After Lomond perhaps Loch Awe is Scotland's premier pike water and it has provided great sport to many over the years. The loch has large pike – the record is currently 38lb 6oz. The big weights are achieved by the pike's feeding on the numerous, large, brown trout that are resident. Some huge ferox trout also co-exist with the pike and the British record is often broken here. My advice would be to focus on the larger reed bays from either the shore or boat. Livebaiting is allowed, but use only fish caught in the loch itself. There are, however, some restrictions on lure fishing – no lures shorter than 5in may be used (although this is not a problem for the big lure enthusiast) – and trolling for pike is restricted to the trout season (15 March to 6 October). My piking partner Graham Barstow's favourite venue was Loch Awe and I shall let him relate his experiences there in his own words:

I started to fish Loch Awe many years ago and it has been one of my favourite places. It has everything you could wish for – dramatic scenery, peace and tranquillity, little competition at the time and it produced. In the 1980s Awe was a venue that pike anglers' dreams were made of and I feel extremely privileged to have experienced the wonder of the place at its best. Those of you who have visited the loch will share my appreciation of this magnificent water. I have driven the whole 26 miles length of the loch and it is very impressive. My favourite area turned out to be the bay at the north end, overlooked by Kilchurn Castle and the dominant peak of Ben Cruachan in the background.

My first trip was attributable to the unmistakable Gord Burton, 'The Piking Pirate'. I had seen an article featuring him holding a large, double-figure pike and the caption beneath read, 'One of Loch Awe's few large pike'. My suspicions were aroused, as perhaps there were many pike as opposed to a few. As a result, I decided to find out for myself what the real potential might be. I gained the interest of my regular piking friends and together we made the necessary arrangements for a trip.

At the end of September we hired a van and set off on the long drive north. We resisted the temptation to fish Lomond, which was also producing good fish at the time, but continued on, arriving, as it turned out, at Kilchurn Bay for first light on Friday morning. It was purely down to luck that we arrived here as we had no any prior knowledge as to where to start. We managed to park the van off road, just up from the castle and I will never forget my first views of the loch. There was the great bay, the castle, the mountain … and the water just screamed pike! We walked down the bank, literally fighting our way through the trees before setting up camp for the weekend. We plumbed the water's depths and found 22ft with a gentle cast. Our baits were mainly mackerel sections, roach, perch and trout, and, once they were cast out, it did not take long for the pike to show. Fish had been topping in front of us earlier as we arrived and a couple of large fish had crashed on the surface. One of them might have been John Metcalf's first pike, which scaled 17lb 8oz. She fought like fury and looked magnificent. Next up and shortly after, John caught a 23lb 12oz to mackerel head, which was to be the biggest fish landed that weekend. I say 'landed' since a number of fish were lost which, in true pike anglers' words, were 'much bigger' than John's best.

The weather was kind to us over the three days. It was warm and sunny, with the water flat calm for most of the time. Generally, these may not be the best conditions for pike fishing, however, it made no difference on our trip. The weekend closed as it began with us still catching. We landed over twenty pike, including eleven doubles, the like of which I had never previously experienced. This was surely a piker's paradise, but could it last forever?

As a result of the first successful visit, I made two trips a year in May and September during successive years. We caught more large pike, with no fishing restrictions to hold us back.

We purchased live trout from farms in the local area and took advantage of all the fishing freedom without abusing it. We took great care with all the pike caught since we respected them and their surroundings, and we also felt we were making an investment for future trips. Then, in May 1992 the Loch Awe Improvement Association (LAIA) introduced day tickets to the venue that restricted pike anglers to two rods only. This was not a real problem, though, as the pike were still willing to be caught and the LAIA were doing some excellent work in cleaning up and promoting the area as a fishery and general tourist attraction.

Unfortunately, as a result of the publicity and promotion, more and more anglers started to visit the loch and they were all eager to get a slice of the pike action. Rows of brollies and bivvies started to appear and catch returns became less over the next few years because of all this fishing pressure. Another problem was that a minority of the anglers were not as caring and responsible as they should have been. Fires and litter

ABOVE: Tony Walker casts into the big, blue yonder of Loch Awe.

Sadly no longer with us, John Metcalf shows off a lovely Awe pike of 23lb 12oz.

abounded and the pike suffered from abuse and mishandling. In addition, many good fish were killed for the pot. This was indeed a sad state of affairs, one which unfortunately has blighted many other Scottish lochs.

Luckily, times change and things have now improved. Although still a popular venue, Loch Awe still fishes well and produces some big fish. I would encourage any pike angler to visit the loch and give it a try. In my view, being afloat is the best way to fish these days and boats can be hired with engines from various points on the water. Loch Awe is still an 'Awesome' place, but for me the idyll of the 'piker's paradise' unfortunately disappeared some years ago.

Turning to Menteith, many will remember this water exploding on to the pike scene when it opened its doors to the PAC some years ago. Because of the continuing large catches it remains a venue that puts big grins on pike anglers' faces. During my role on the PAC committee I attended some of the lure events to help to run things even though they were not really my cup of tea as I am more of a deadbaiting man. Anyway, the lake took my breath away on my first visit; not exactly 'awesome', like some of the wilder, mountainous lochs, but really, really bonny. I fished it three times as a committee member and with very good lure men such as Mark Leathwood, Dave Foster and Dave Lumb. Although I thoroughly enjoyed these days, I failed to catch and instead yearned to find a feature and try my deadbaiting skills.

I fancied a go in 2003 but did not have a like-minded boat partner. However, in 2004 Chris Parry accepted an invitation to have a go and, being a lucky Welshman, he secured us a boat on the bait fishing day in spring 2005. After a relaxed evening with some old PAC friends in the Rob Roy pub, the following morning we made our even more relaxed preparations to load the boat ready for the day ahead. In fact, I think that we were the last ones away. Chris had a good idea where to fish as he had bait fished here successfully before and, after 10min careful depth-finder monitoring, found a nice, reef-like feature to anchor off. We both deployed our deadbaiting

tactics and awaited the action which, as it turned out, soon came. During the morning we both caught steadily, jacks and low doubles that fought like hell. We also lost a couple apiece too.

In the afternoon things stepped up a gear as we both got stuck into more doubles, with Chris doing well with a 17lb 4oz and a 20lb 4oz, which he nearly returned unweighed until I convinced him that it was bigger than he thought. Handshakes in order, we then continued to haul fish and, though now smaller pike, the sport was steady and satisfying. But I was still awaiting a biggie.

During mid-afternoon the wind really picked up as I returned a fit thirteen pounder for Chris. Then, as I was having a tidy up, I had to jump on to my left-hand rod as it bounced off the middle seat with the clutch screaming. The take was so fierce I did not see the float go under. Chris thought I had made a crazy grab for him and said the look on my face was amazing as I lunged. I then struck into what I knew was my best fish so far. After a few hefty runs, the fish came up at the boat side and Chris gasped, 'That's a big 20 if not a 30 Steve.' I said a little private prayer to myself ... 'keep calm lad.' We quickly decided whether to net or let Chris chin her and, since I trusted Chris, he skillfully double-handed a big pike over the gunwale. We both knew that it was a 30-plus and, as I lifted the Reubens scales, they bounced between 32 and 36lb due to the big waves, so I settled and was very happy with 32lb. Things were obviously now working to plan.

It got a little hairy as I released her. I did not want to let the fish go too quickly so I nursed her bulk at the side of the boat. She was happy to stay where she was and so I did not let go in case she had trouble. As the waves slapped at my face and my hands started to freeze, unbeknown to me the front anchor had lifted and the boat was starting to spin sideways. Chris was getting anxious, but then, fortunately, the fish slowly slipped away and swam under the boat.

I then added a big jack and an eleven pounder to the tally while Chris struck into and lost a decent fish and then had a big jack too. Things went quiet for a while as the wind abated. We managed to regain our senses and have a hot

ABOVE: A cracking 20lb 4oz for Chris Parry from Lake of Menteith.

drink. Later, as we started to pack up for the return to the boathouse, Chris's rod was away and he connected with a lump. As the fish came to the net we both thought that it was another 30 because of her deep flank, but we were amazed when the scales read 25lb 8oz. Still, Chris was not complaining. On the way back we both thought that there must be a few other good catches and big fish since we had done so well. However, we were surprised to hear that most of the boats had blanked or caught very little. Nevertheless, it goes without saying that it been a very memorable day's fishing for me in great company while also experiencing some of Scotland's finest scenery. The pint surely tasted sweet that evening.

Before leaving central Scotland we must mention the Kinross region, which is often overlooked in preference to some of the more famous waters. However, it has a lot to offer the visiting pike angler. There is the mighty Loch Tay, with its famous river, running south west to north east from Killin to Kenmore. There are also lochs Rannoch and Tummel just a little further north, and another productive water Loch Errochty up above the Tay forest. Finally, to the south of the region is Loch Earn. Although, as I have mentioned, these lochs are often neglected in terms of pike fishing they all hold the potential to produce fish to the specimen size.

Steve Ormrod's chunky Lake of Menteith 32lb, which fell to a float-ledgered half sardine.

The Highlands

We now come to the Highlands and they start at its gateway of Fort William off the main arterial A82. To me, once you pass through 'Fort Bill' you really are moving into the prime of Scotland's scenery and the pike fishing can be very good too. Let us begin with the Lochaber area. Although there is not a lot of water here, two lochs are worth a mention. Nestled in Glen Spean is Loch Laggan, off the A86, and a little lower down is the north–south running Loch Treig. Both are worth a visit and contain pike. There are a lot of smaller waters in the area but most are very inaccessible, although no doubt they contain pike since many are linked up to the Laggan–Spean river system.

But arguably the cream of the Highland's piking exists in Glen Mor, the Great Glen. It is headed by the greatest mass of freshwater in Britain, namely Loch Ness, followed south westwards by lochs Oich and Lochy. The three are linked by the Caledonian Canal, which is worth fishing in itself. To the west lies the wild and remote Loch Arkaig and to the east of Ness are several smaller, shallow lochs such as Ruthie, Tarff, Mhor, Duntelchaig and Knockie.

I have paid a few visits to Loch Arkaig over the past ten years as it is one of those waters that both inspires and gains respect from the individual.

When the westerly winds blow hard off the Sound of Sleat and down Glen Pean she becomes a wild and unforgiving place indeed, such that, when there is a 'big blow' on the loch, it is hard to find anywhere to hide. All this reminds me of a trip Ken Macdonald and I once had. On arriving at Arkaig after the long drive north, we spotted a nice looking bay with several burns running in. Plumbing revealed a decent, sloping drop-off not far out, with shallows to the right and deeper water to the left. Ken set up to the left of the bay with his baits near the deeper water, while I opted for the drop-off and the shallower area. Two of my rods were set up on either side of the burn inlet since there was a superb sandbar where the currents had deposited silt and pebbles. It went out about 30yd, gradually sloping away before dropping to over 60ft. I carefully placed baits along the sandbar edges right and left in about 16ft as they neared the deeper water. This proved to be a good choice, but before we fished we decided to have a couple of hours' kip since we had been on the road for nine hours since midnight. Before this I lobbed in some chopped-up freebies around the sandbar in preparation for the afternoon and evening's fishing.

Rubbing the sleep from our eyes, we got the baits in before rustling up some late lunch. We had spotted trout splashing in the oxygenated top layers off the drop-off, right near to the baits,

Another of Steve Ormrod's piking partners Ivan Fletcher, with a trout-caught Loch Oich double.

this giving us confidence. Soon enough, Ken had a roaring take on a joey but did not connect with it. We concluded that it was probably a mad trout. I had decided to leave my baits in the same place for a few hours and lobbed in a few more chopped freebies every now and then. Later on in the evening the tactics were to pay off. One of the sandbar rods got a couple of bleeps and the rod tip bounced, so I quickly unclipped the drop-back. As I did, the loop of braid in my hand almost sliced into my palm as a hard run developed. I made connection with my first Arkaig fish, which gave me a really hard fight while I was imagining all sorts about its size. Amazingly though, all we netted was a lean 12lb 8oz torpedo, with a huge forked tail. I was still very impressed to say the least.

I later added another low double and lost another fish. After lashing in some more freebies I left Ken on guard while I had a doze in the bedchair. It was surprising that, although Ken's baits were nearby, he did not get any runs. An hour later I took the vigil and Ken got some shut-eye as the skies darkened. I then decided to twitch one of my baits up the sandbar in case any fish were patrolling closer in. Moments later the sandeel roared off in good style and this time I was convinced that I had a very good fish on. Many searing runs without seeing the pike again got me thinking 'monster', until an angry, mad double flung itself clear of the surface shaking its head. The result was a superb 15lb 4oz and, size for size, never had I encountered such hard-fighting pike. Soon though it was dark and the action ceased as we enjoyed a dram or two under the stars before bringing the baits in and retiring to the bivvies.

We were up again at first light to get the baits back in. It was a dull morning surprisingly and it had the threat of rain in the air. Soon after breakfast one of my 'sandbar' rods was away again, leading to another crazy scrap off an 11lb plus. Unfortunately, the weather then turned for the worst as a howler of a westerly blew in off Sgurr Thuilm, the Munroe in Glen Pean which funnels the Atlantic winds in. The fishing became impossible as 4oz leads were being bounced around in the crashing swells and undertow. The beautiful Arkaig had become a beast.

We decided to make a run for it before the rain arrived and went off to find a more sheltered spot higher up the loch that Ken had fished before. It was here that he witnessed a friend spectacularly lose the fish of a lifetime as it smashed his rod due to a tight clutch. 'We'll have some of that', I said (the fish, I meant). However, the next two days and nights were spent just trying to survive in the horrendous weather that saw the loch levels rise by at least 4ft due to the big Atlantic squall. What were calm, bubbling burns were turned into raging torrents that burst their courses and spilled out across the flatter bay areas. We would have been swamped out if we had stayed in the original burn swim.

Fishing was difficult and we struggled to present baits to feel in with a chance. Still, we ate like kings to keep our spirits up and on the fourth day we awoke to a lovely dawn. The storm had

A Loch Arkaig 14lb 12oz fish for Steve Ormrod.

broken and we set our stall out for some action once again. It became quite hot and sunny and, although the trout were there and it was fun catching them for lives, no pike succumbed. So, as the weather had settled, we decided to break camp and try the first swim again. This time I made Ken fish the burn on the sandbars since I had done so well there and yet he had not landed a pike. However, the sport did not return, probably as a result of the storms, although Ken did get a tearing run on the morning we packed up ... from a ferox. All the way home, and even to this day, that Arkaig trip amounts to great memories of one of my favourite lochs.

Another area with many big waters and potential is Glen Garry. The main Garry system starts in the west, with the frightening Loch Quoich and its huge dam wall. As you head east into Glen Garry itself, you follow the River Garry, which gradually widens until it spills into the very picturesque Loch Garry, another inspiring water. Above Glen Garry are Lochs Loyne and Cluanie off the A87, Kyle of Localsh road. All contain pike although the fishing can be hard at times. Further east, in Strathspey, at the foot of the spectacular Cairngorm mountain range, there are several waters well worth attention – lochs Alvie, Beag and Insh (on the River Spey), Loch Pityoulish (boat fishing only) and the mirror-like Loch Morlich, on the way to the Cairngorm ski centre. Loch Alvie in particular is well worth a try, not least because it is legendary for its massive 49lb 11oz pike caught by Col Thornton in about 1784. It is a natural glacier loch nestled between the spectacular Monadhliath and Cairngorm ranges. Despite some recent reports of gill netting, good pike are present but, as always, location is the key to success.

We now come to Wester Ross in the northern Highlands and things get a little more difficult because, in truth, this area is largely unknown in terms of pike fishing. Admittedly many of the lochs are acidic and lack nutrients and so pike do not always thrive, but lochs a'Chroisg (Rosque) and Crann definitely have potential for pike, along with Sgamhain, Clair, Coulin and Dughaill. A little further north is the huge and beautiful Loch Maree, which must have some pike present even though it is a known game water. Further east you will find lochs such as Luichart and Achanalt, and in the south of the region are the frighteningly grand, rugged lochs Monar and Mullardoch. It is all very wild country, indeed, and, as indicated, the pike fishing still remains to be fully explored.

Rivers and Canals

Having dealt with some of the main Scottish lochs, it is timely to turn to the rivers and canals. Scotland has some superb river systems, for example, one has only to think of the Spey and the Tay. They all contain pike to some extent but, sadly for the pike angler, some of the most promising stretches tend to be salmon beats and are exclusively private. However, with a little hard work and polite research I am sure that some good fishing could be found. Furthermore, I suspect that the potential could be frightening, with pike over the 30lb mark surely being a possibility. But it must be remembered that access can easily be obtained on some rivers such as the Bladnoch in the west of Dumfries and Galloway.

You should not underestimate the potential of the Scottish canal and waterway systems. There are several to note for the visiting pike angler. First, there is the Union Canal, which stretches for 32 miles between Edinburgh and Falkirk. It has easy access from the many roads that crisscross it. Next, the Forth and Clyde Canal is a magnificent feat of civil engineering that cuts across the central belt of Scotland, traversing city centres, suburbs and some remote and beautiful countryside. It links the Forth to the Clyde, allowing boats to sail across Scotland from the North Sea to the Atlantic. And then there is, as already mentioned, the Caledonian Canal, an amazing Highland waterway that links the Moray Firth in the north east at Inverness with Loch Linnhe in the south west at Banavie. The canal itself is only about 25 miles long, but links the sea at each end by running, as mentioned, through the Great Glen, linking

Steve Ormrod and a Caledonian Canal 14lb 6oz.

up lochs Ness, Oich and Lochy. All contain good stocks of pike, with 20lb specimens being a real possibility.

Tactics, Rigs and Baits

Let us now turn to a discussion of tactics, rigs and baits. At the outset it must be noted that Scotland is a place where you need to be flexible in the way you fish each water. Obviously, if it is a water that you have fished many times you will have a good idea of what to expect and what tactics, rigs and baits will work. Most of the tactics and rigs I use for bank fishing in Scotland are much the same as those described in Chapter 7 since such pike fishing can be pretty similar. Consequently, a lot of the time I will bait fish with a float-ledger rig because I feel that this is the safest method when there is a danger of submerged rocks or sharp drop-offs. A loop of weak mono is a must on the ledger link, just in case it gets snagged up. Large, unloaded pencil floats are also essential to counteract the big wave swells that often occur on the larger lochs. For distance, I use a simple ledger rig made up of trace, snap-link, pushover soft buffer bead and run ring with a weak mono loop attached to a 3oz ledger. Lures also accompany me to Scotland because I find it therapeutic having an hour or so covering a weed bay, this being a break from

static bank fishing. The lures used vary from Bulldawgs and spinnerbaits to small replicants and spoons. In all these approaches the key is to find the right hotspot, this, in turn, depending on the time of the year. For instance, springtime will find a lot of pike still in the shallower bay areas after spawning and, if you catch them post-nuptial, you can have fantastic sport. Indeed, as a starting point, bays adjacent to large points are a good place to be, especially if deep water is close by. Pike will patrol the drop-offs for prey and have to go around points to reach the bays too. But do not think that the bays are always the best option, since fishing shallower shelves on a point can also be productive. Perhaps a good compromise is to pitch camp in one of the bays and have a morning or afternoon fishing off one of the nearby points. Always look for main arterial burns running into the bays since they are great hotspots for pike. The trick is to fish the sloping sandbars on either side of the inlets where the silt deposits have accumulated, much as I did during the Arkaig trip.

As for baits, I tend to take sealed packs of baits that can survive a bit of thawing such as joey mackerel, lamprey, eel and launce. I also take smelt, trout and sardines, which I use up first because they do not survive long. Trout livebaits can often be sourced from local fish farms and you can always catch your own although this can be difficult at times.

Although I enjoy bank fishing the lochs, perhaps the best way to fish these often big, open and wild waters is from a boat with a good echo-sounder to locate the drop-offs and reefs. Trolling can be a good method, either with baits or lures, as are 'drift and cast' tactics with lures too. Many pike anglers are content to find a particular feature with prey fish present and then anchor up and fish static baits. Most lochs have launching facilities for those bringing their own boats, but it is always best to check beforehand, and do not simply launch without permission. Many of the waters hold trout and have boats for hire anyway.

When you look at the rivers you can easily see why the piking potential is so great. Scottish rivers are basically game fish spawning grounds, with salmon preferring well-oxygenated, silt-free water where they will rest in deep pools on their way to the higher spawning grounds. These same deep pools are also the haunts of old esox. It is also worth noting that Scottish rivers are well fed with rainfall so they stay quite deep in the lowland areas. This is where sport is at its best, especially where the rivers widen too. Some rivers have almost 'lochan' style deeps, such as Loch Ken, where the surrounding land has been flooded with a main channel running in the deepest part.

As for the canals, being 'sea-linking' they are designed to take some large vessels so they tend to have good depths with the main channels being kept clear of too much silt and debris. For the pike fishing, normal canal tactics work, for example, static fishing the 'wides' or more mobile approaches such as rod-hopping and sink-and-draw or lure fishing the regular stretches. Although most areas may seem barren of features, they do produce fish. Even so, features such as bends, overhanging trees and bushes, moored ships, boats, barges and pontoons are likely to be key hotspots. But by far the most productive areas are the 'wides'. Out of the main channel they tend to be good prey-fish holding areas. These wides can be quite large with depths up to 20ft or more and they often have good weed beds, thereby supporting a decent food chain and making them ideal places for pike.

In short then, I hope that this chapter has given you an insight into the pike fishing in Scotland. But remember, fishing in magnificent scenery and wildlife, together with the thrills and spills of fishing with like-minded companions, is a precious resource. This must be respected, protected and conserved for the future. So to coin a phrase or two, 'leave nothing from your stay, only take away good memories – *sláinte*!'

A top tip for pike fishing Scottish lochs is to fish the burn inlets.

11 PIKE FISHING ON THE BIG WATERS OF IRELAND

Mark Ackerley

Ireland, and by this I mean the Republic of Ireland and Northern Ireland, is a fascinating place to visit. There are the delights of towns and cities such as Dublin, Cork, Galway and Belfast, bewitching villages, ancient ruins, lively pubs and the gregarious Irish people. Once visited, the Emerald Isle is never forgotten and this, of course, equally applies to the pike angler.

What is it then that makes Ireland such a Mecca for pike anglers? It is quite simple really. There are lots and lots of waters, loads of food fish and, best of all, relatively few pike anglers. This situation can only result in good, at times great, pike fishing. One has only to recall the numbers of Irish 35lb-plus fish that have been caught. For example, Lough Conn has produced many such fish, topped by John Garvin's 53lb monster, albeit that was in 1920. More recently loughs Corrib and Mask have produced many pike to over 40lb, including Ottoman Airing and Bert Rozemeijer catching forty-two pounders in 1996 and 1995, respectively. When it comes to rivers mention has to be made of the Shannon and the Suck, which between them have produced pike to over 40lb. And then there are numerous other loughs such as Carra, Ree, Derg, Sheelin and Ennell, which have all produced leviathan pike.

Admittedly, there is a view among some pikers that Ireland is not the place it once was. While this may be true of certain venues, on the whole, I am of the belief that the standard of pike fishing in Ireland is currently far better than that in England, and I can certainly say that the keen Irish pike anglers and regular visitors that I know seem to do very nicely indeed.

In this chapter, as the title states, I largely deal with pike fishing on the big waters of Ireland, not least because these are the ones where I tend to spend much of my time. Thus I begin by looking at venues, this being followed by sections on tackle and tactics, and boats, as these form the main way in which I would pike fish in Ireland. I then deal with the Irish piking year, a when-to-go piece, if you will. But, despite the optimism of some of the above comments, I also look at some of the problems confronting pike fishing at the present, but I end on an upbeat note by describing a very successful session that led to a new Irish personal best.

Venues

If you just take a look at a map of Ireland you will see that there are an awful lot of blue bits. These range from the mighty Shannon system and associated loughs to the great western loughs, some of which have already been mentioned. Then there are hundreds if not thousands of smaller loughs, many rivers and the canals, not least the Grand Canal. It is not surprising that the pike angler is spoilt for choice.

One of the hardest parts about recommending places to pike fish in Ireland is that things do have a habit of changing rather quickly. Take the western loughs, for example. In the mid-1990s it would not have been far off the mark to say that Lough Mask offered possibly the best big pike angling in Europe, but since the gill nets returned from 1997 onwards the same cannot be said today. Then the Bann system, with Lough Beg in particular, really looked like it was becoming the place to go a few years back. Sadly, a major fish kill has left the venue a shadow of its former self. Or again, Lough Allen was a

A stunning brace of Lough Corrib 20s taken by Mark Ackerley on simultaneous runs.

Peter Robinson, Mark Ackerley's companion on many Irish trips, with a Lough Mask twenty-nine pounder.

favourite venue for both locals and visiting pike anglers for many years, yet piking results declined and these days few seem to bother with it. But pike fishing does go in cycles and it can take only a few years for things to turn around. What was once a good pike venue can bounce back, especially if pike-angling pressure is reduced, so do keep an eye on those waters that disappear from the news for a few years. Loughs Corrib and Mask are the classic examples of the forgotten venue bouncing back. When the gill netting was at its peak in the 1970s and the 1980s pike anglers naturally gave them a wide berth. However, when the gill netting ceased around 1986 pike anglers were very slow to clock on and a handful of keen English pike anglers and I had the loughs nearly to ourselves for five years, until the word began to spread. It was pike fishing of a standard that I doubt I shall ever see

again. Sadly, just as the pike were getting seriously big the gill nets returned and it was back to square one.

So what then are we looking for in our choice of venues? First of all I would look for one with a good head of food fish for the pike. I would also be looking for a large venue, whether it be river or lough. Although even tiny venues can produce big pike, they are far more susceptible to pressure. For a big catch of fish we need a decent area of water. For me that would start at a couple of hundred acres and go up to as big as they get. If access is difficult, with poor bank fishing access or a lack of slipways, then that is even better. Many pike anglers still look for a venue where they can park their car and walk a short distance to their swim. The harder it is to get to the swim, the smaller the pike angling pressure will be and the better the pike fishing

145

usually is. Distance from Dublin can also be a factor: the population demographics are such that a very large percentage of the population, and therefore of the pike anglers, live in the Dublin area. Those venues within easy travelling distance of Dublin certainly get a lot more pressure than those further away.

The British angling press can be a good source of information on venues that are producing lots of pike food in the form of match or pleasure catches. The Irish angling monthlies are also worth keeping an eye on, as is the Irish Pike Society (IPS) magazine for more specific pike-angling information. Hugh Gough's book *Coarse Fishing in Ireland* (*see* Further Reading) is worth obtaining, if it can still be found, although the information is now a little out of date. The Internet can be a very useful tool; several of the Fisheries Boards have their own website, the Shannon Regional Fisheries Board being by far the best. But do not try looking for coarse fishing information on the Western Regional Board's site since it is preoccupied by game fishing.

I have also found the information produced by the tourism authorities to be of use. For example, the Midlands-East Regional Tourism Authority publishes an excellent brochure on pike fishing in the midlands of Ireland. It deals with the River Shannon, Lough Ree, Lough Forbes and the River Inny, including Lough Derravaragh and the Gowna network of lakes. Included are useful tips and other snippets of information, for example. Lough Ree has productive pike fishing on the western shore at locations such as Blackbrink and Galley Bay and from Portrunny Bay to Lanesborough, or, on the Shannon, it is pointed out that the wider stretches are most productive, including such as above and below Clonmacnoise, at the junction of the River Suck and River Brosna and around Meelick.

Tackle and Tactics

Let us now take a look at the tackle that would accompany me on an Irish trip. Starting with bait rods, I have to admit to making a complete U-turn in the last few years and I have swapped from using rods of 12ft in length to ones of 10ft for all my boat fishing. The shorter rods will cast as far as I need to and are so much easier to handle in the boat and car. As nearly all my piking in Ireland is done from a boat, these rods will be all that I would take. For me, Dave Lumb's 3lb test curve and 10ft Loch Tamers are perfect for the job. They will cast the biggest baits that I would use and the steely action certainly seems to help in setting the hooks. A further plus point is that they seem to be just about indestructible and cope well with the bumps and bangs of being chucked about in the car and the boat. Mine are custom-made with full duplon handles, which I find help in holding the rod securely in a boat rod rest.

One thing to bear in mind is that, under Irish regulations, you are limited to the use of two rods only. In fact, you are supposed to have a maximum of only two rods with you at a time. This second point, I think, is just daft. I would normally have with me three bait rods and a lure rod, but I guess discretion should be the name of the game. To partner the rod, the choice is either a multiplier, usually an ABU 6501 or a fixed-spool baitrunner model. There are plus points for both types of reel, but generally I prefer a baitrunner, the Shimano 10000 XTE being the best that I have used. To go on the reel I would always use a braid. Having tried all types of braid over the last few years, I keep going back to Power-Pro, which I think is unmatched. For bait fishing that will be 65lb breaking strain. Traces are made from Fox Carboflex in 30lb; this is the most durable trace wire I have ever used. On my last Irish trip I had the same traces on for almost the entire two weeks. Treble hooks will be Owners in size 2 or 4 or the Fox 2XS treble in 4.

As regards the tactics for bait fishing, we are, of course, limited to the use of deadbaits only. This presents the keen pike angler with a dilemma since baits are so easily caught on many Irish waters, particularly during the warmer months, and you can easily be tempted to use them. However, my own view is that it just is not worth

A nice 24lb fish for Mark Ackerley; part of a huge haul of pike taken on float-trolled deadbaits from a bay on a western lough.

BELOW: *Mark Ackerley and the classic lines of a Mask 30, a battle-scarred 30lb 12oz.*

the hassle, particularly as deadbaits are so avidly consumed on all the Irish waters I have fished. In addition, time spent catching fresh bait is also time wasted for pike angling. So deadbaits it is, and for me these will either be fished static, float ledgered on the bottom, or float trolled, a method that does seem to be more successful during the warmer months. The choice of deadbait for static fishing usually revolves around a half mackerel and something else, probably a smelt, trout or lamprey. When the pike are really up for it, mackerel are unmatched; however, at times the pike do seem to prefer something a little more subtle. I never cease to be amazed at how pike can show a preference for one type of bait, so I always offer a choice until a trend emerges. For float trolling, a medium-sized herring would be my first choice, with natural baits being used if dropped takes occur. On most of the venues I have float trolled in Ireland I have never found the need to fish the bait deep, even over deep water. The pike seem willing to come up for the bait and so a float set at around 6ft will suffice in most situations.

For the visiting angler a means of keeping your deadbaits frozen during the trip is essential. When choosing accommodation the first question I ask will be about freezer facilities. If adequate facilities are not available then I will take a small freezer with me. This is a risky option, though, as freezers do not take well to being moved in vehicles. To get the deadbaits to our destination they will be packed tightly in large, polystyrene boxes; a smaller, polystyrene box is used for keeping the day's supply of bait frozen in the boat, a far better method than most cool boxes or bags.

Lure fishing for pike in Ireland does seem to be increasing in popularity, as it has in the United Kingdom over the last ten years and with good reason too, since on its day it can be a devastating technique. I must admit to not having done much lure fishing in Ireland back in my earlier Lough Mask days. I was a fervent bait angler and perhaps a little blinkered in my ways. However, in recent years, having done a lot of lure fishing on the British trout waters, I have

taken the methods to Ireland and caught a few good fish, including my best ever Irish pike, as we will see.

The lure rod will be a 6ft jerkbait rod, partnered with an ABU 6501 multiplier, with which, at a push, I can chuck most of the lures I want to. Again, Power-Pro braid is used but this time in 80lb breaking strain. If space permits, I may take a lighter 9ft rod with a fixed spool and 50lb Power-Pro for casting lighter lures, especially spoons. The top of my list of favourite lures for Irish piking would have to be a spoon and, for me, that would always be a Kuusamo Professor spoon. There is something almost magical about these lures and I know others who have found the same. I use mostly the two largest sizes, 0 and 00, and, as for colour, it really does not seem to matter much. Kuusamo spoons can be trolled, but I much prefer to cast them, particularly from a drifting boat using a drogue to slow the drift down if required. Running a close second to the Kuusamo for me are Bulldawgs and Squirrley Burts. Bulldawgs should need no introduction to most readers; they are made of rubber, which pike all over seem to love. I would take a selection of the large Magnum Dawgs and the standard Bulldawgs, including a few of the lighter weight Shallow Dawgs. My view is that Bulldawgs have to be the easiest lure to fish ever; you simply cast them out and wind them in again. The standard-weight Dawgs are best suited to waters of 10ft-plus depth, but for waters of less than 10ft my first choice would have to be a Squirrley Burt. For me, the Squirrley Burt is one of the best lures of all for triggering a pike to take. They are floating lures, which dive when retrieved. They are best fished with short 18in pulls then a pause. The pause is the key, because, as the lure hangs there, the rubber grub tail keeps on wriggling for a short while. Many of the takes seem to come on the pause, so do stay alert is my advice. A weighted Squirrley should be able to go to 6ft on the retrieve. Regrettably, most of the lures produced in recent years do not seem to be weighted sufficiently and need some DIY attention to get them to perform to their full potential. If I saw

Lough Corrib in an evil mood; although Mark Ackerley rarely bank fishes, when the weather gets this bad it is the only option.

BELOW: Calmer conditions; sunset on a western lough.

an active pike in shallow water and had to choose one lure to cast it would be a Squirrley every time. I hardly ever seem to get follows on Squirrleys, the reason, I think, is that the pike grab them first time rather than follow them. It was the situation of seeing a pike swirl on the surface and then casting a Squirrley at it that produced my biggest ever Irish pike on one of my recent visits. To complete my lure selection I would probably take a few flipper-type jerk-baits, such as Cobbs Crazy Shads, Slappers and some trolling lures, such as Shad Raps and Invaders. Of course, in reality I would usually take a far greater selection, but I do not honestly think that I would miss out by taking only the lures mentioned here.

To complete our tackle line up I would also take some banksticks, my Delkim alarms and drop-back indicators for the rare occasions that I do end up fishing from the bank rather than a boat. On certain of the Irish rivers we will use the boat to get to the spot, then disembark and fish from the bank. This allows a better spread of the rods and improved bite indication. It is also nice to be able to stretch your legs.

Boats

As I mentioned earlier, almost all of my Irish piking is done from a boat. I certainly would not even think about travelling to Ireland to pike fish without the use of one, and, in fact, many of its waters can be effectively fished only from a boat because of poor bank fishing access. Take the Shannon above Meelick Weir and the lower River Suck as an example: the water level in this area is regulated by the weir and in the winter the water is often way over the fields and without a boat you would struggle to get anywhere near the main river channels.

Boats also give you the advantage of being able to move quickly from spot to spot without the rigmarole of having to pack up. My standard routine is to fish a spot for an hour to an hour and a half maximum, then move on to the next one. Usually if you are going to catch you do so

very quickly. Many times I have had an immediate take before I could even get a second rod out. It goes without saying that moving swims in this manner is so much easier from a boat. But a downside to piking from a boat is, of course, that you have to get it there. This adds considerably to the ferry cost and makes the journey longer. Irish roads are generally far worse than roads in the United Kingdom and to tow a boat in some of the rural areas can be a nightmare. Trailers have to be up to the job, and do make sure that your boat is not going to be damaged as it bounces around on the trailer.

It is worth mentioning that many Irish slipways are a bit rough and ready and you may need a vehicle with fair pulling power to avoid getting stuck. I am currently driving a Toyota Rav4 4×4 and this means that I can launch in some places where a car would struggle.

As to the choice of boat, for years and years I made do with an Orkney Spinner, usually with a 4hp outboard. The Spinner is a stable fishing platform but its speed is not a strong point. It takes time to get from spot to spot and this is time that could be better spent actually fishing. The answer naturally is a faster boat and, having spent some time fishing from boats with 30 to 40hp engines over the last few years, I am now a convert. Faster boats also enable you to run from bad weather, an important safety point when one considers how the weather can suddenly change for the worse, not least on the larger loughs.

My ideal Irish pike fishing boat would be between 14 and 16ft in length, with a planing hull, although not of the flat-bottomed, cathedral hull type. It would have a folding cuddy and a small casting deck at the front. The folding cuddy gives much more space in the boat than a fixed cuddy and makes anchoring and trolling much easier. On the back of the boat would be an engine of at least 20hp, ideally a 30hp four-stroke. A small petrol or Minn Kota electric engine is used as an auxiliary and for trolling. To go with the boat, a good quality trailer with plenty of rollers is required, preferably a breakback model.

The choice between glassfibre or aluminium is up to the individual. Glassfibre boats are much more stable, but are heavier and therefore harder to launch and a bit slower than a comparable aluminium model. If I had to recommend a couple of models they would be an Orkney 440 or 520 in fibreglass or a 14 to 16ft walk-through Sea Nymph in aluminium. Even so, the best boat in the world is not much use if you cannot hold anchor in a bit of a blow and so anchors of decent quality are essential. The best I have seen are my mate Chris Bolton's home-made ones. Of the commercially available types I would recommend a 10kg Bruce with about 6ft of heavy chain and 100ft of anchor rope. When anchoring up, the anchors are held on long ropes front and rear, tightening up to each

as much as you can. This should hold the boat securely and also make it a lot easier to deal with a fish that dives under the boat.

Boat rod rests are also an essential item. The plastic John Roberts type rests are the ones I favour, my boat being fitted with six permanent fixtures to hold the rests in different positions. A good quality sounder makes life a lot easier particularly when trolling. Mine is a Lowrance X102C colour sounder, an amazing bit of kit. This is powered by a good quality 12V deep cycle battery, one of two that I have in the boat. The other will power the electric trolling motor. After all, it is always worth having more rather than less battery power available, just in case you end by having to use the electric motor to get home in the event of main engine failure.

An ideal Irish piking boat; Mark Ackerley's mate, Chris Bolton, with his 16ft walk-through Sea Nymph.

A large, round boat fishing net is kept permanently assembled in the boat. You really do not want to be frantically assembling a net when a large pike is wallowing on the surface by the side of the boat. The new Fox boat landing net is spot on. When a large fish is netted it is held in the net over the side of the boat while forceps, sling, cameras and so on are readied. If you have to put a pike down in the boat then make sure that it is well cushioned with a large, soft, unhooking mat.

An auto-inflating life jacket is also required, although really it should be seen as the last line of defence. It is important always to take care to listen to a weather forecast before setting out and, if things look dodgy, then, although it might be stating the obvious, take care to avoid risks. As much as we love catching pike, they are not worth risking your life for. A mobile telephone is always carried for safety reasons and a hand-held GPS can be very useful on the largest waters.

The Irish Year

Having got your tackle and boat sorted out, it goes without saying that timing your trip to Ireland right is of great importance, particularly if it involves using a week of precious annual leave from work. Starting off with spawning time, it is my experience that Irish pike spawn a few weeks earlier than their English cousins. Spawning pike are not good news for the angler since this usually coincides with their switching off from feeding. The second week in February is as late as I will usually leave it for a visit. Post-spawning is a traditional time for a visit and many people choose April for their annual pilgrimage. The pike at this time can be well up for it and will usually be in shallow water and feeding on the spawning coarse fish. The downside is that the pike may be lean and out of condition. Personally, I prefer to leave things until May when the pike should be packing on the weight again.

Some readers will be aware that I am not a great fan of summer piking. On several Irish venues that I know, however, you do get large concentrations of fry at the end of August and early September and this can result in prolific fishing as the pike exploit the food source. I now prefer to leave the summer months to other pursuits and October is usually as early as I would consider an Irish trip, but November through to February is my favoured time for a visit. The fair-weather pike anglers will have disappeared, as will have the holiday makers in their cruisers. As a result you should be able to find peace, solitude and, not least, the pike should be in peak condition and ready for some action.

The Dark Side

But, despite some earlier comments, there are many serious threats to pike and pike angling in Ireland. First and foremost has to be the systematic destruction of pike by gill netting by the Fisheries Boards on the large 'trout' loughs, particularly those in the west. As I mentioned earlier, major gill netting on the western loughs of Corrib and Mask resumed in 1997 and continues to this day. Although each year a few big pike are caught by pikers, you are really up against it and you will be fishing for only a handful of big fish in a large water. It can be hard going indeed, and perhaps life is too short for this.

In 2004 a review was held by the Central Fisheries Board on pike angling in Ireland. All the concerned parties were invited to participate. The pro-pike corner was defended vigorously by the IPS and assisted by the Pike Anglers Club (PAC). The conclusions gave a glimmer of hope: the recommendation was for a cessation of gill netting on loughs Corrib, Conn, Cullen and Sheelin, with gill netting to continue on Mask, Arrow, Ennel, Owel and Carra. But sadly, as I write this in March 2005, there is still large-scale gill netting taking place on areas of Corrib. Only time will tell what the real future will hold but there are obvious concerns here. In the meantime, please add your support to the fight against the gill netting of pike in Ireland by joining the IPS and the PAC. For only the cost of a couple of meals or a few pints in a pub you will be doing your bit to ensure the future of pike angling. Details of how to join the IPS and the PAC can be found on their websites.

Pollution is also a problem affecting certain Irish venues. As the urban centres continue to expand and new houses appear every year in many country areas, the pressure on sewage systems becomes ever greater. Lough Corrib is one place where this effect can be seen: water quality in lower Lough Corrib, at the bottom of the water chain of the Corrib system, is poor due to the concentration of sewage from the many houses on the banks. This can be seen in the condition of the pike, which are lean and many show infestations of *Argulus* lice. This is in contrast to the pike at the head of the Corrib system, which are generally much better conditioned, fatter and lice-free.

Furthermore, as the popularity of pike fishing continues to grow in Ireland, the effects of inexperienced pike anglers can be widely seen. A good friend of mine, a regular visitor to Ireland, reports that on all his recent visits he has caught several pike with traces in them. On my last trip I personally caught about six fish with broken gill rakers. Both are symptoms of poor pike angling. The education process is a slow one, but the Irish monthly magazines are doing their bit, as are the IPS.

Pike matches form, I am afraid to say, another threat. Although the policy is to return pike alive in nearly all of these matches, the standard of angling seen and, in particular, the methods used to retain pike are of concern. In some matches, believe it or not, 200ltr drums cut in half lengthways are used to retain the pike in the boat until they can be taken to a central weighing station. A mate who used to spend some time on Derravaragh Lough a few years back told me that it was common to see dead and distressed pike the day after the matches, and as well as Fisheries Board-condoned netting, illegal netting by poachers is also a problem. On the whole, this seems mainly to be confined to the Bann system and loughs around the north–south border. However, recently I have seen reports of illegal nets found on Derravaragh.

To sum up: with gill nets, pollution, poor pike angling practice, pike matches and illegal netting, Irish pike certainly have a lot to contend with. But, despite this, you can still have some excellent sport, as I hope the following shows.

An Irish Piking Session

It is 4 a.m. and time to get up. We are five days into our two-week trip and the weather forecast suggests that the time could be right for a visit to the big lough. We grab a quick coffee, fill the cool box with deadbaits, load the car, hitch on the boat and set off. Nothing stirs at this time of the morning in Ireland. We pass through deserted towns, the only sound being the banging of the boat on the trailer as the potholed roads do their worst. We do hope that the trailer lasts. What is more, we have already lost a trailer board off the back and had a winch post shear off on this trip. But Chris is at the wheel and so I can relax as we chat about the prospect ahead of us. We have three days planned on the venue and, although it is bit of a long shot in some ways, you have to try these things from time to time. Having already had loads of sport on the trip, we can easily cope with a blank.

Two and a half hours later we arrive at the slipway. We made good time and dawn is still half an hour or so away. Our friend Neville is already there, fast asleep in his pick-up truck with the engine still running. He wakes as we pull up and gets out to greet us. He looks pleased with himself and not surprisingly. After four days' struggling he had taken a brace of 20s the day before. Things certainly seem to be looking up.

The Sea Nymph is quickly launched and, by this stage of the trip, we really have the routine down to a tee. Not 15min after arriving we are ready to 'rock and roll'! Nev is still pottering about, but we are impatient and so it is time to go. Chris starts the 30hp Mariner up and we are soon on the plane, hurtling to the fishing ground. I love this bit – bracing wind on the face and full of eager anticipation of what the day might bring. When we arrive at the chosen area we start up the

The rods are out at dawn on an Irish lough.

sounder and have a quick look around. Nev's fish had come while trolling and casting lures, but we know exactly where we want to be and so static deadbait fishing it is for us. Chris positions the boat and we drop the anchors on long ropes front and rear. There is 12ft of water, with reeds an easy cast on one side of the boat and open water on the other. The usual float-ledgered baits are cast out; nothing special, these being a half mackerel each, and a sardine for Chris and a lamprey section for me. The waiting begins, so it is time to get the kettle on and have a hot drink. We sit back, relax and enjoy the moment. The conditions look perfect as it is overcast with a gentle breeze. In the distance we can see Nev on the troll. It is his last day so he is working hard, but we are going to sit it out all day on the spot. If this fails we can always go on the troll over the next couple of days. Two hours or so pass and I then take a small fish on the lamprey section. At least it is a start, we say to ourselves. Every half hour or so one of us has a few casts around the boat with a lure, but nothing shows any interest. At around 10a.m. I am on the casting deck, throwing a Squirrley Burt, when Chris announces that a fish has just swirled at my deadbait float. I turn around and watch my float with expectancy. I think to myself that surely it will go under? I wait a short while but then cannot resist casting my lure at the float. After a couple of pulls the lure is snatched, but it does not feel as if it is a big fish and I relate this to Chris in a matter of fact sort of way. 'But your rod is really, really bending!', Chris exclaimed. The as yet unseen pike dives under the boat and I have to sink the rod deep and pull it back. I catch a glimpse of a sizeable tail as the pike powers off again, feeling bigger by the second. Then it surfaces by the boat and I am soon shouting at Chris to get it in the net, which he quickly does. I have lost it by now as the fish is not just big, it is huge! Chris holds the fish safely in the net over the side of the boat while I fumble about for scales, sling, camera and the unhooking gear. The fish is quickly hauled into the boat and on to the unhooking mat. It looks perfect with not a blemish to be seen. Almost certainly it had never been caught before, and you will not be surprised to know that I was really chuffed with myself. On the Reubens scales it was a fantastic feeling as a weight of 34lb 8oz was recorded, an Irish personal best some fifteen years after the last one. Chris then does the honours with the camera, taking some fine pictures, as we see when later they turn out. Soon the fish has been returned and we are like a pair of schoolboys, laughing at the sheer joy of it all. It was what we had come for and all the planning and preparation had come good. It is moments like this that I live for.

Another pike was caught some half hour or so later, though unsurprisingly not in the same league as the previous one. And then Nev came past us and we tell him what he had just missed. He was impressed to say the least, but, as he was going home soon, he is soon back at his trolling, trying to make the most of those precious last few hours.

As good as it gets? A magnificent 34lb 8oz Squirrley Burt lure-caught Irish personal best for Mark Ackerley.

A chunky 20 from an Irish river for Mark Ackerley, which fell to a float-ledgered deadbait.

That night in the pub we are celebrating, of course. Soup starter, then seafood platter for me with a few pints of the black stuff. It is a nice thought that I have just caught a bigger pike than the cased specimen over the fireplace. Who knows, there may be further cause to celebrate again after the next couple of days' fishing?

However, two days later a couple more jacks turned out to be the disappointing tally. Even so, we head back to base camp still on a high. With over a week of solid pike fishing still ahead of us there is plenty to look forward to. Not least there are new venues to explore. A 20 from that river would be nice ....

FURTHER READING

Bailey, J. and Page, M. (1985), *Pike: the predator becomes the prey* (Crowood Press)

Brown, M. (1993), *Pike Fishing: The Practice and the Passion* (The Crowood Press)

Davies, C. *et al.* (2004), *Freshwater Fishes in Britain: the species and their distribution* (Harley Books)

Fickling, N. (1986), *In Pursuit of Predatory Fish* (Beekay)

Fickling, N. (1992), *Pike Fishing with Neville Fickling* (Freshwater Publishing)

Fickling, N. (2002), *Everything You Need to Know about Pike Fishing* (Lucebaits Publishing)

Fickling, N. (2004), *Mammoth Pike* (Lucebaits Publishing)

Gough, H. (1989), *Coarse Fishing in Ireland* (Unwin)

Moules, D. (2003), *The Fenland 30s – A History of Fenland Pike*

Palmer, B. (2005), *Dimples to Wrinkles and Beyond* (Arima)

Philips, D. (1990), *Pike* (Beekay)

Pike Anglers Club (2000), *Pike Fishing beyond 2000* (PAC)

Rickards, B. (1992), *Success with Pike* (David & Charles)

Rickards, B. and Gay, M. (1987), *The Pike Angler's Manual* (A. & C. Black)

Rickards, B. and Whitehead, K. (1987), *Spinning and Plug Fishing* (Boydell Press)

Tetley, L. (1998), *The Yorkshire Dales Angler's Guide* (Cicerone Press)

Tetley, L. (1999), *The Lake District Angler's Guide* (Cicerone Press)

Turnbull, C. (1990), *Big Fish from Famous Waters* (David & Charles)

Wilson, J. (1995), *Where to Fish in Norfolk and Suffolk* (Jarrold Publishing)

Winship, B. (ed.) (1990), *Pike Waters* (Boydell Press)

USEFUL ADDRESSES

Irish Pike Society
website: www.irishpikesociety.com
Ian Forde, general secretary
email: ian.forde@irishpikesociety.com

Lure Anglers Society
website: www.lureanglers.co.uk
for membership contact: Bob Tweedle
15 Craneley Road, Groby, Leics LE6 0FD
tel: 01162 914776
email: roberttweedle@beeb.net

Pike Anglers Alliance for Scotland
website: www.esoxecosse.com
Steve Tapley, general secretary
email: steve.tapley@esox.ecosse.com

Pike Anglers Club
website: www.pacgb.com
John Cahill, secretary
email: secretary@pacgb.co.uk

Pike Flyfishing Association
website: www.pikeflyfishing.co.uk
for details contact: Peter Jones
28 Crown Avenue, Holbeach St Marks
Spalding, Lincs PE12 8EU
email: pjn276@aol.com

Staffordshire Predator Angling Group
website: www.predator-group.co.uk
for details contact: Charles Sargent
tel: 01782 751571
email: enquiries@predator-group.co.uk

INDEX